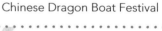

March

1   St David's Day (National Day, Wales)

17   St Patrick's Day (National Day, Ireland)

21   New Year/Naw-Ruz (Baha'i)

Mothering Sunday

Holi (Hindu)

March/April

Easter (Christian)

Passover (Jewish)

April

13/14   Baisakhi (Sikh)

23   St George's Day (National Day, England)

May

1   May Day

23   Anniversary of the declaration of the Bab (Baha'i)

May/June

Whitsun/Pentecost (Christian)

Shavuot (Jewish)

Wesak (Buddhist)

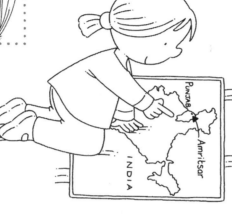

June

16   Martyrdom of Guru Arjan (Sikh)

Chinese Dragon Boat Festival

July

9   Anniversary of the martyrdom of the Bab (Baha'i)

July/August

Raksha Bandhan (Hindu)

September/October

Harvest (Christian)

Rosh Hashanah (Jewish New Year)

Navrati (Hindu)

Yom Kippur (Jewish)

Sukkot (Jewish)

November

Birthday of Guru Nanak (Sikh)

12   Anniversary of the birth of Baha'ullah (Baha'i)

24   Martyrdom of Guru Tegh Bahadur (Sikh)

30   St Andrew's Day (National Day, Scotland)

October

Simchat Torah (Jewish)

October/November

Kathina Day (Buddhist)

Diwali (Hindu/Sikh)

RE: What you must teach

The Education Reform Act 1988

In 1944 the Education Act made the teaching of religious instruction a legal requirement in Britain. At that time religious instruction was perceived to be Christian only as this reflected the population of the country.

Since the 1960s, however, racial and ethnic shifts in population have meant that in some areas children in schools are from a variety of religions and creeds and from many different parts of the world. RE advisers and teachers recognised this and interpreted religious instruction liberally, including the study of non-Christian religions in their syllabuses.

This recognition was finally enshrined in law with the Education Reform Act 1988 which stated that every local authority should have an agreed syllabus, locally determined, which must 'reflect the fact that the religious traditions in Great Britain are in the main Christian, whilst taking account of the teaching and practices of other

principal religions represented in Great Britain', in other words Hinduism, Judaism, Buddhism, Islam and Sikhism.

This was reiterated in the Education Act 1996 which made religious education part of the basic curriculum for all children in schools. The foreword to the non-statutory national framework for RE opens with the words:

> 'Every pupil in a maintained school has a statutory entitlement to religious education.'

This remains the situation in England and Wales today. Scotland has slightly different requirements with RE being incorporated into RME (religious and moral education). RME has been acknowledged as one of the eight curriculum areas that should inform curriculum planning in Scotland's Curriculum for Excellence which was introduced in 2005. (For more information visit www.educationscotland.gov.uk)

In England and Wales all children have the right to receive religious education which is non-confessional and non-denominational (we are not trying to convert anyone to any particular religious viewpoint) but aims to inform children and young people of a variety of religious standpoints.

Some agreed syllabuses also include non-religious life stances such as Humanism or other faiths not mentioned in the Act, particularly where these are found in the area. This requirement has been endorsed by the non-statutory national framework for RE (published in 2005) which states:

> 'To ensure that all pupils' voices are heard and the religious education curriculum is broad and balanced, it is recommended that there are opportunities for all pupils to study:
>
> ● other religious traditions such as the Baha'i faith, Jainism and Zoroastrianism
>
> ● secular philosophies such as Humanism.'

Unlike subjects in the National Curriculum, each local authority produces its own agreed syllabus, so called because it has been agreed by a conference consisting of representatives of the faiths in that community: teachers; local authority officers and the Church of England. Syllabuses are often backed up with schemes of work or guidelines and training will be provided by the local authority to support the syllabus and its implementation. They may also include guidance on RE in the early years.

Faiths and Festivals Book 1:

A guide to the religions and celebrations in our multicultural society

by Christine Howard *et al.*

CONTENTS

Published by Practical Pre-School Books, A Division of MA Education Ltd, St Jude's Church, Dulwich Road, Herne Hill, London, SE24 0PB.

Tel: 020 7738 5454

www.practicalpreschoolbooks.com

© MA Education Ltd 2012. Revised 2013.

Design: Alison Cutler **fonthill**creative 01722 717043

Illustrated by Cathy Hughes.
Front cover images, main picture © iStockphoto.com/Nicole S. Young, other images (top to bottom) © iStockphoto.com/Murali Nath,
© iStockphoto.com/Liubov Tokareva and © Rafael Ben-Ari/ Fotolia. Back cover images (left to right) © iStockphoto.com/ DistinctiveImages, © iStockphoto.com/MKucova, © iStockphoto.com/kaczka.

ISBN 978-1-909280-58-8

JOSEPH PRIESTLEY COLLEGE

25823

Calendar of festivals

Guidance on dates

Different religions have different calendars – for example, the Jewish calendar is based on the traditional date of creation. Each Jewish year contains 12 lunar months of 29 or 30 days.

Islam on the other hand dates from the flight to Medina, al Hijrah in 622. It is a lunar calendar so the Muslim year shifts back in relation to the Western calendar. The first of the month is determined by the sighting of the moon in Makkah. Eid ul-Fitr falls at the end of the month of Ramadan.

Buddhist festivals are even more complicated because the dates vary from country to country and between different Buddhist traditions. So while many Buddhists celebrate Wesak on the first full moon day in May (except in a leap year when it is in June), others, for example Tibetan Buddhists, celebrate it in June.

If this seems daunting, check out the date with a couple of sources. Useful websites include:

- www.reonline.org.uk/supporting/festivals-calendar

- www.shapworkingparty.org.uk

Try to use more than one source from the religion you are looking at. If there is still no agreement and you have families from that faith in your group – ask them. This is a quick and easy way to obtain the information, it takes into account any local traditions and is a wonderful way of involving parents in the work you are doing.

January

1   New Year's Day

6   Epiphany (Christian)

6   Orthodox Christmas (Christian)

January/February

Chinese New Year

The Muslim lunar calendar

The Muslim year is 354 days divided into 12 months of either 29 or 30 days long. Because the lunar year is shorter than the solar year on which the Western calendar is based, Muslim holy days cycle backwards through the Western calendar. The number in brackets indicates the number of the Muslim month, for example Ramadan is the ninth month.

Muslim festivals

Muslim New Year – 1 *Muharram* (1)
Safar (2)
Muhammad's Birthday – 12 *Rabi'al-awwal* (3)
Rabiulakhir (4)
Jamadilawal (5)
Jamadilakhir (6)
Night Journey of Muhammad – 27 *Rajab* (7)
Shaban (8)
Eid ul-Fitr – end of month of *Ramadan* (9)
Shawwal (10)
Zulkaedah (11)
Eid ul-Adha 10-13 *Zul-Hijjah* (12)

February/March

Shrove Tuesday (Pancake Day) (Christian)

Ash Wednesday – first day of Lent (Christian)

Purim (Jewish)

December

Advent

25   Christmas (Christian)

Bodhi Day (Buddhist)

Hanukkah (Jewish)

December/January

Birthday of Guru Gobind Singh (Sikh)

Expressive arts and design

- Within this area religious stories and ideas provide a wealth of material for children to be imaginative by exploring thoughts and feelings through design and technology, art, music, dance, role play and stories.

For more information on the EYFS, visit: http://www.education.gov.uk/schools/teachingandlearning/curriculum/a0068102/early-years-foundation-stage-eyfs.

Although RE is not specifically mentioned as a separate subject, the Early Learning Goals require that children from the age of three in the Foundation Stage will:

Personal, Social and Emotional Development

- Have a developing respect for their own cultures and beliefs and those of other people.

- Understand that people have different needs, views, cultures and beliefs which need to be treated with respect.

- Understand that they can expect others to treat their needs, views, cultures and beliefs with respect.

Knowledge and Understanding the World

- Begin to know about their own cultures and beliefs and those of other people.

The Foundation Stage

The Education Act 1996 applies to all registered pupils in Reception classes and above. Nursery classes are not subject to the requirements of their local agreed syllabus. However, this does not mean that these children are exempt from any form of religious education.

The Early Years Statutory Framework became mandatory for all early years providers from September 2012 and although RE is not specifically mentioned as a separate subject, religious topics have an important role within the Early Learning Goals **prime** and **specific** areas.

Within the **prime areas**:
Communication and Language

- Listening and attending: children listen attentively in a range of situations. They listen to stories…

- Understanding: children … answer 'how' and 'why' questions about their experiences and in response to stories and events.

In the **specific area**:
Understanding the world

- People and communities: children … know about similarities and differences between themselves and others, and among families, communities and traditions.

Useful books and websites

- *Understanding World Religions in Early Years Practice* by Jennie Lindon (Hodder and Stoughton) ISBN 978-0-340-74786-5
- *Shap Book of World Festivals* edited by Alan Brown (RMEP).
- *Shap Calendar of Religious Festivals*, published annually by the SHAP Working Party on World Religions. For further information visit: www.shapworkingparty.org.uk
- www.theredirectory.org.uk
- www.reonline.org.uk
- The national framework for religious education: www.mmiweb.org.uk/publications/re/NSNF.pdf

Learning about festivals

For most people involved in teaching religious education to young children, festivals are an easy way in, though they are not the only way in which RE should be delivered.

Learning about festivals helps children become aware of a variety of cultural and religious beliefs, symbols, customs and traditions in a non-threatening and enjoyable way.

This book covers a number of religious festivals which you may wish to incorporate into your planning. It looks at the origins of some of the festivals you are most likely to come across, how they are celebrated within the faith communities, the stories associated with these festivals and includes some suggestions for activities to try out with your children.

If you are going to explore religious festivals with your children, once you have chosen the festival, there are a few things that you need to check out before you begin:

- What is the nature of the festival? What is it celebrating? Make sure that this is clear in your own mind, for example is it a type of harvest festival; a new year celebration or a commemoration of a significant birthday or event?

- What is the underlying meaning of the festival? Does it celebrate particular themes, for example light in darkness; overcoming evil? Understanding at this stage will help to avoid the mistake of mixing up festivals or explaining one in terms of another. For example, Eid ul-Fitr is not a Muslim Christmas. The former celebrates the end of the fasting month of Ramadan, the latter the incarnation of Jesus, whom Christians believe to be the Son of God.

- What are the stories associated with the festival? Stories are a good way of introducing a theme or consolidating work which has been done. They also provide a wealth of material to base activities around.

Try to vary the activities so that there is always something fresh to maintain children's interest. Do not be tempted into making these activities compulsory as this may alienate some children and prevent spontaneous learning. The best learning happens when children are interested and engaged. Remember that you do not have to be an expert on everything to do with religion but a little preparation can help you avoid the more obvious pitfalls.

Christine Howard

Choosing a festival

- Talk about marking festivals rather than celebrating them. Some parents may be concerned if they think their children are celebrating a festival which is not part of their religion. Marking a festival conveys that it is an important event for some people but that it is not something they personally celebrate.

- Be aware that festivals, like religions, may be inextricably bound up with a particular tradition and culture. The celebration of the festival may vary from culture to culture or the festival may even be celebrated in a secular way. Christmas is an example of this, where there are wide differences in Christmas customs and these may be celebrated by Christians and non-Christians alike.

- Do not feel you need to cover every festival. Be selective. Find out the festivals which your families are most likely to celebrate and then add some of the other significant ones. Choosing a few unfamiliar festivals as well will allow both children and adults to share in the learning experience.

Working in a global environment

There are some complex issues to confront if you want to take a truly multicultural approach.

The family living next door to me is Irish Catholic. The neighbour on the other side has a Hindu father. Next door but one is a Jewish family, then a Buddhist family from Thailand and a West Indian family. At the back of my house are Jewish and Muslim families whilst opposite me lives a young Sikh couple. I am married to a Welsh man with a Jewish father. My grandmother was Canadian but can trace her ancestry to German settlers and I have Scottish blood on my mother's side!

This is the sort of society in which children are growing up. Even if they live in predominately 'white' areas they will meet this global community through travel, books and television. The phrase 'global village' is a reality. It is our role as educators and parents to equip children to participate and delight in this shrinking world.

The role of religion

Yet a global culture brings many complex issues of which we need to be aware. These include race; language; differing attitudes to sex and sexuality; cultural identity; customs; traditions; belief and, of course, religion. However, whereas many educators are happy to embrace a multicultural approach to their work, they shy away from anything to do with religion. This may be because they are afraid of offending another's religious sensibilities or because they themselves have no time for religion. For some, who stand within a religious tradition, it may stem from a belief in the truth of their own particular standpoint and a reluctance to admit to the validity of others.

Nevertheless, many who hold a religious belief are unable to separate their faith from their culture and their whole way of life. One obvious example would be food and dietary laws. A British Muslim might well enjoy roast beef and Yorkshire pudding, as long as the beef is halal (permitted) but neither Jew nor Muslim will sit down for an English breakfast fry-up of sausage, egg and bacon, if they observe their religion's food laws. Such dietary restrictions are not based on a whim but have their origins in religious belief and are dictated by a divine authority. Failure to understand this can lead to stereotyping, misunderstanding and insensitivity.

When the multicultural approach ignores the role of religion it can be characterised as 'saris, samosas and sandals' – a concentration on the outward signs of difference rather than what makes people who they really are.

If religion is central to many people's lives, then we have to be aware of this and educate ourselves and the children in our care so that they can learn to respect and understand the life stances of others and why they behave as they do.

- Everything you do should aim to encourage active respect between children, parents and teachers.
- Do not indoctrinate.
- Be open with parents: keep them informed and consult them. Where you have families from different faith backgrounds, encourage them to be involved and share in your activities.
- Always be positive.
- Avoid tokenism, the 'exotic' and stereotyping.

Create a multifaith/multicultural environment by:

- Having welcome posters in a variety of languages (you might like to try using some other forms of greeting as well, such as 'namaste').
- Using pictures and posters from a variety of religions, cultures and countries.
- Incorporating different types of foods into your activities (check on dietary restrictions first).
- Using stories from a wide variety of traditions and cultures.
- Including culturally different artefacts and clothes in your home corner or dressing-up box (check first for any cultural/religious sensitivities).
- Listening to music and songs from a variety of traditions and cultures.
- Encouraging visits to places of worship and different communities.
- Being aware of what the festivals or major religious events are for the children in your group and encouraging them to share this with the rest of the group.

The Baha'i faith

The Baha'i faith is the most recent of the world religions and has followers in more countries than any other, apart from Christianity, yet it is perhaps one of the least known.

The Baha'i faith was founded nearly 160 years ago, in Persia (now Iran), by Baha'u'llah, a Persian nobleman. His father was a minister of the Shah and most people thought that his wise and caring son would follow in his footsteps. Instead, he turned away from worldly power and followed the teachings of a messenger of God called the Bab ('the gate'), who taught that the time had come for the appearance of 'the promised one', who would revitalise the world.

Baha'u'llah (meaning 'the glory of God') was imprisoned shortly after the Bab was executed for his beliefs. In prison, God revealed to him that he was the promised one, for whom all religions were waiting. For the next 40 years, he was a prisoner and an exile in Palestine until he died in 1892.

During his exile, he wrote more than 100 volumes of scriptures and prayers, including letters to kings, queens, presidents and religious heads throughout the world. He asked them to turn towards God and justice for humanity and away from earthly power, riches and tyranny.

Today there are more than six million Baha'is from every nationality and culture. After Christianity, it is the most widespread faith in the world. According to the Christian Science Monitor of September 1998, the Baha'i faith is the seventh largest faith in the world at 6.1 million. There are 15,021 Baha'is in England and Wales according to the 2011 census.

Between 1868-1873, during his imprisonment in Akka, Palestine (now in Israel), Baha'u'llah wrote letters to the rulers of the world.

To Napoleon III in 1869, he wrote: 'For what thou hast done, thy kingdom shall be thrown into confusion, and thine empire shall pass from thine hands ...' Within a year, Germany defeated France and he was overthrown.

To Queen Victoria, he wrote: '... thou hast entrusted the reins of counsel into the hands of the representatives of the people. Thou indeed hast done well ...' Queen Victoria said: 'If this is of God it will endure, if not it can do no harm.'

Hers was the only positive reply from the kings and rulers.

Basic beliefs

Baha'u'llah taught certain principles which were revolutionary at the time, but are now generally recognised as a civilised and enlightened way of living.

Baha'is believe that God is one, that all the world religions come from the same God, and that humanity is one. All prejudice (racial, national, religious, sexual) should be abolished, science and religion should be in harmony, and women and men should have equal rights, opportunities, and privileges. If any part of humanity is prevented from achieving its potential then, like a broken-winged bird, it cannot progress as a whole.

For Baha'is, oneness is the centre of the faith. They call for humanity to unite and live peacefully together. Baha'u'llah wrote:

● 'The earth is but one country and mankind its citizens.'

● 'So powerful is the light of unity that it can illuminate the whole earth.'

● 'Ye are the fruits of one tree, and the leaves of one branch.'

There are no restrictions on what Baha'is can eat, but they believe that, eventually, everyone will eat only what is grown from the earth.

Ready for unity

Baha'is believe that in every age (every 500-1,000 years) a new messenger, or manifestation of God, comes to refresh humanity spiritually. The spiritual teachings of loving God, loving each other and following God's will are the same in each religion; the difference is in the social teachings, which are suited to the age in which each new manifestation reveals his teachings.

Every manifestation is treated with equal respect by Baha'is because they are, in essence, one. The manifestation is the perfect reflection of God and the Holy Spirit that comes from God is in each one of them. Even though their physical appearances and personalities are different, their spiritual qualities are the same.

Worship and prayer

Baha'is should read the writings of Baha'u'llah in the morning and in the evening. It is vital that they reflect upon what they have read, so that they understand what is being asked of them.

Baha'is have a choice of daily obligatory prayers, but there are many hundreds of other prayers that may be said for different occasions and purposes.

Every month Baha'is in each community have a feast, which is a meeting in three parts: the devotional, where scriptures and prayers are read; the administrative section, where community activities are discussed; and the social section, where light refreshments are served by the host. In smaller communities, feasts take place in people's homes; in larger communities, halls may be hired or a Baha'i centre may be bought and used.

There is a Baha'i house of worship in every continent. Although they all look different, they have certain things in common. Each one has nine sides to represent the nine world religions. All are open to any person of any religious belief to come and worship in their own way. Inside, the only instrument allowed is the human voice. All reflect something of the culture in which they are based. For example, the Indian house of worship, in New Delhi, is in the shape of a lotus flower, surrounded by pools of water. The lotus is an important symbol in Indian life: a sign of purity that stands above the muddy waters in which it grows.

Education

Education for all was supported by Baha'u'llah in the mid-1800s, so it is important to Baha'is. Baha'i children are taught to respect and investigate other religions so that they can understand other people better. They are not restricted from taking part in collective worship and – unless they are shy – would be pleased to share their prayers or short quotations they have learned by heart, which are universal. Baha'is do not believe in making images of the messengers of God, so it is better not to ask the children to do so.

The Baha'i calendar

The Baha'i calendar has 19 months, each with 19 days, which makes 361 days in total. To make this up to 365 days (366 days in a leap year), there are days of hospitality, called the Intercalary Days, between the 18th and 19th months (26 February-1 March).

There are a number of holy days, on nine of which Baha'is should refrain from working. Some of the most important are: Ridvan (21 April), the day when Baha'u'llah declared his mission; the Declaration of the Bab (23 May), the forerunner of Baha'u'llah; and Naw-Ruz (21 March), which is New Year for Baha'is worldwide and all Iranians.

The days of hospitality serve an important purpose: they are a time for community sharing and gift giving, as well as a preparation for the forthcoming fast. Baha'is fast from 2-20 March (the last month of their year) during the sunrise to sunset period. Children under 15, pregnant women, sick people and people over 70 do not have to fast.

The fast is a time for prayer and reflection, when Baha'is consider their strengths and shortcomings and determine to improve themselves.

Administration

Baha'is have no clergy and no ceremonial ritual of any kind, as they are encouraged to search after truth for themselves. No person can intercede between them and God, except for his manifestation.

However, the Baha'i faith does have an administration. This was ordained by 'Abdu'l-Baha, the son of Baha'u'llah. He was given the title of the Perfect Exemplar of the Faith. His life was that of a perfect Baha'i: all the qualities Baha'is aim for, such as universal love, kindness, justice, consideration, trustworthiness, discipline, patience, simplicity and fortitude were embodied in him. Before he passed away in 1921, he wrote a will and testament which was a blueprint for the administration.

'Abdu'l-Baha also wrote in his will that his grandson, Shoghi Effendi, should be the guardian of the Baha'i faith and that all Baha'is should turn to him for guidance. He led the faith for the next 36 years and guided the Baha'is to develop the administration laid out in his grandfather's will and testament.

At his passing in 1957, he left no will, so the 'Hands of the cause of God' (men and women who had been appointed by the guardian himself) looked after the affairs of the faith until 1963, when the Universal House of Justice was elected, the international body specified in the will and testament of 'Abdu'l-Baha. The Universal House of Justice has the right to make and change new laws, in the gaps deliberately left by Baha'u'llah, so that changing world circumstances could be catered for. The House of Justice cannot change or interpret the writings of Baha'u'llah, 'Abdu'l-Baha or Shoghi Effendi.

There are local and national assemblies all over the world, and the Universal House of Justice in Haifa, Israel, which guides the world community. The local and national assemblies are elected by secret ballot, and without any electioneering or campaigning, every year. The House of Justice is elected in exactly the same way, once every five years, by the national assembly members.

Baha'is make decisions through a process of consultation. This means that any ideas offered to the group for discussion no longer belong to the individual who suggested it: the idea belongs to the group, which can accept, reject or modify the idea. This avoids the problem of individuals taking over and disunity arising. It allows for a variety of viewpoints, but when a decision is made, everyone has to abide by it. Baha'is believe that an incorrect decision will become obvious if all obey it, and at the next consultation it can be corrected.

Buddhism

The 2011 census indicates 0.4% of the population of England and Wales are Buddhists.

Buddhism began 2,500 years ago with the experience of a young man named Siddhartha Gautama, who was born in northern India. He left a wealthy and privileged life of comfort to search for the answer to a pressing question: why do people suffer?

After much meditation, fasting and study with spiritual teachers, Siddhartha realised that the answer to his question lay within the depths of his own mind. Tradition tells that he sat down in the shade of a tree to meditate. Sitting there, still and deep in concentration, he eventually experienced 'Enlightenment' – a total transformation of his whole being and world view. He knew that he now understood 'the way things really are'; the cause of suffering, and the way out of suffering. From then on, he was known as the Buddha – 'One who understands the truth'.

Basic beliefs

At his Enlightenment, the Buddha saw that there was no creator God, no external authority, but that we live in a vast network of interdependent conditions. Everything depends upon everything else and when one thing changes, lots of other things change, too. All events, including our own actions, have far-reaching consequences, even if we cannot see them.

Although we like it when unpleasant things come to an end, we generally don't like change and ending. Whether it's that our parents are separating, or our ice cream is all gone, it makes us feel anything from insecure to just disappointed. Everything in life, no matter how lovely, is temporary, and this is hard to accept.

Everything would be fine if we could just face the fact that this is how things are and learn to love life as it is. Instead we try to avoid this reality by looking for security in new experiences and new things: better games and toys, more sweets, different friends. But we soon get disappointed again, or bored, and then we look around for something else to fill the gap.

Suffering, said the Buddha, is caused by our endless craving for new things or experiences. It is possible, gradually, to bring this to an end. But it takes training. To lessen our craving, we need to develop a tranquil appreciation or acceptance of the things we have. This tranquillity rests in part on developing a clearer conscience by living a kinder, more ethical life. More ethical behaviour and a deeper appreciation of every moment both

The Four Noble Truths

At his Enlightenment, the Buddha realised that:

- We all experience suffering.
- Our suffering is caused by greed and selfishness.
- There is a way to stop this greed and selfishness.
- That way is the Noble Eightfold Path – a list of areas of life in which we can learn to live more in accordance with 'the way things are'.

require greater awareness, which is why Buddhists meditate. Through ethics and meditation, the Buddha taught, every one of us can make progress and eventually become wise and compassionate – Enlightened – just like him.

The Three Jewels

At the heart of Buddhist life are the Three Jewels: the **Buddha**, **Dharma** and **Sangha**.

The Buddha represents Enlightenment, the total fulfilment of human potential. Buddhists believe that by his own example, he proved that any human being can eventually attain Enlightenment.

The Dharma means the teaching of the Buddha, by which Buddhists live:

- the 'truth of the way things really are', and also

- the teachings which lead to a total understanding of 'the truth'.

The Sangha is the community of those living by the Buddha's teachings, across the world and throughout time. Some Buddhists use this term to refer only to monks and nuns.

In pre-schools and nurseries

Since Buddhism does not include worship of a creator god, you should avoid assuming that all religious believers share belief in God. Buddhist children should not be expected to take part in collective worship centred on God.

If you have any Buddhist artefacts, books or Buddha figures, explain that they should be handled with care and respect.

Diet

The first of the five ethical guidelines which all Buddhists recognise is to avoid killing, and to be kind to all living things. Some Buddhists live out this principle through what they choose to eat, and are vegetarian or vegan. However, this is always a matter of personal choice, and some Buddhists are not vegetarian. There is no such thing as typical Buddhist food (or dress); Buddhists eat (and wear) whatever is customary in their culture.

Revere
Buddhists revere the Buddha, who represents the Enlightenment they, too, seek to reach. When they offer reverence, or simply bow to a Buddha figure, they are giving thanks for the Buddha's life and teaching and reminding themselves that they want to follow it. They do not worship him as a god.

Meditation
There are many different forms of meditation, but all enable the development of a calm state of mind and body, and lead to greater awareness of oneself, others and the world around us. In turn, this makes it easier to understand 'the way things are'.

It is not considered good practice to teach Buddhist meditation to children in a group, out of respect for those of other faiths or none. However, 'stilling exercises' can be beneficial. These can involve visualising somewhere beautiful, listening to taped music or noises such as bird song or the sound of waves on a shore. Such activities can result in calmer, more positive states of mind and increased concentration spans.

Scriptures
Buddhists have no one scripture. There are hundreds in many Asian languages and the earliest set of scriptures – known as the Pali Canon – is about 26 times the length

of the Bible! The best-known single volume is the Dhammapada. The scriptures are treated respectfully and not usually placed on the floor, but they are not regarded as the word of a god, or as an infallible record of the Buddha's teaching.

Holidays and festivals
Buddhist festivals vary around the world, with many being particular to one country. The most commonly celebrated is **Wesak**, or Buddha Day, which falls on the full-moon day in May. This marks the Enlightenment of the Buddha and, for some Buddhists, also his birthday.

Political sensitivities
It's a common misconception that all Buddhists are of Asian descent; 39 per cent of UK Buddhists are white British converts and 4 per cent are black or mixed-raced converts. Since the 1960s there has been a great interest in Buddhism in the West, where Buddhism is now the fastest-growing religion.

In India, where Buddhism died out shortly after the time of the Buddha, there has been a significant Buddhist revival. To escape their low-caste status, hundreds of thousands of Hindus previously considered 'untouchable' and now known as Dalits, have converted to Buddhism (and other faiths). There are Indian Buddhists in parts of the UK, for example in west London and the Midlands. You should be aware of possible sensitivities between Hindus and Buddhists of Indian descent.

It is also traditional for Hindus to regard Buddhism as part of Hinduism and the Buddha as a manifestation of the Hindu god Vishnu. Buddhists do not accept this.

Buddhists have their own dating system, but tend for practicality's sake to use the conventional Western calendar. Like many non-Christians, Buddhists use the terms Common Era (CE) and Before Common Era (BCE) rather than AD and BC.

Munisha, education officer, The Clear Vision Trust

The five ethical guidelines
- To avoid harming living things, and to cultivate loving kindness.
- To avoid taking what has not been given, and to cultivate generosity.
- To avoid sexual misconduct, and to cultivate contentment.
- To avoid false speech, and to cultivate truthfulness.
- To avoid intoxicants which cloud the mind, and to cultivate clear awareness.

The Dalai Lama
The Dalai Lama is probably the world's most famous Buddhist. He is the political leader of Tibet and the spiritual leader of just one Tibetan Buddhist tradition. There is no overall worldwide Buddhist leader.

Useful address
- The Clear Vision Trust, 16-20 Turner Street, Manchester, M4 1DZ. Tel: 0161 839 9579. Website: www.clear-vision.org A Buddhist charity making Buddhist storybooks and videos.

Christianity

Christianity is a worldwide faith with about 2.1 billion followers, making it the largest religion. The 2011 census indicates 38 million of the population of England and Wales are Christian. Christians worship in different ways and have different cultures and ways of organising themselves or denominations but there are core beliefs that hold them all together.

Christianity grew out of Judaism. It traces its origins to first century CE Palestine (modern day Israel), when the young Jewish teacher, Jesus from Nazareth, was crucified by the Romans.

According to the Christian scriptures, Jesus was raised from the dead three days later by God and appeared to his followers or disciples. These followers came to believe that Jesus was the Son of God and yet was fully human. They called him the Christ, which means Anointed One and is the Greek version of the Hebrew Messiah.

The Jews believed God would send His Messiah to save the world. Jesus' followers talked about what they believed and the news spread throughout the Roman Empire. According to the Bible, it was in Antioch that the name Christians, after Jesus' title 'Christ', was first used (Acts 11:26).

The first Christians were Jews but soon non-Jews were also being converted and joined the Church.

Beliefs

The beliefs of the early Church were codified in 381 CE with the formulation of the Nicene Creed. This remains the core beliefs of Christians today. They are:

- God the Father, who created the world.

- Jesus, His Son, who was born of a virgin mother called Mary. This is called the doctrine of the incarnation. He died and rose from the dead to save mankind from its sin.

- The Holy Spirit, God, present in the world and active through his people. (This doctrine of the three aspects of the One God is known as The Trinity.)

- Resurrection of the dead and eternal Life – that Christ will return on the day of judgement, and then the dead will be raised to eternal life with Him. Some Christians believe this will be a bodily resurrection, others see it as more spiritual.

Church

The main Christian day of worship is Sunday, though many Christians meet together at different times in the week for prayer and Bible study and a wide variety of community activities. Children usually attend a Sunday School and may also go to youth clubs during the week.

The Christian place of worship is called a church, though some Christians meet in house groups. Those denominations which have bishops (for example, Roman Catholic and Anglican Churches) also have cathedral churches where the bishop has his throne (normally a wooden seat).

The form of service varies according to the type of church. Common elements in a church service are the singing of hymns, Bible readings, prayer and a sermon or homily in which some aspect of the Bible reading or Christian life is explained.

Sacraments

Most Christian churches, apart from the Salvation Army and Religious Society of Friends (Quakers), have two common rituals which are called sacraments. A sacrament has been defined as 'an outward and visible sign of an inward and spiritual grace'. They are baptism and Communion.

Baptism

Jesus commanded his followers to baptise in the name of the Father, the Son and the Holy Spirit and so baptism with water has become a rite of initiation for a Christian. Most churches baptise children but some, notably Baptists, think that only believers should be baptised and so they wait until the person is old enough to make the decision for themselves. Baptists also baptise by total immersion rather than by pouring water over the head as is common in most churches.

Communion

The rite of Communion, also known as the mass or Eucharist, follows a commandment given by Jesus at the Last Supper which he shared with his disciples before his death. Jesus took bread and wine and told his disciples to 'Do this in remembrance of me' (1 Cor 11:23-26). The frequency with which Christians celebrate it and the way they interpret it varies. Some (for example, Catholics) believe that the bread and wine become the actual body and blood of Christ (transubstantiation) while the non-conformist churches see it as more symbolic.

Scriptures

The sacred writings of Christians are called the **Bible** (from the Greek word for book). This is in two parts. The first is the New Testament comprising of four gospels which tell of the life and teachings of Jesus; the Acts of the Apostles, which tell of the first years of the early church after the death of Jesus, a number of letters from early Christian leaders and the book of Revelation which contains symbolic imagery about what will happen at the end of the world. The second part which Christians also read and study is the Jewish Bible (Tenakh) and they refer to this as the Old Testament. Testament means covenant or promise.

Moral codes

Christians follow the Ten Commandments which are found in the Book of Exodus (Ex 20: 7 – 17) in the Old Testament or Jewish Torah. Jesus summed them up as 'You shall love the Lord, Your God, with all your heart, and with all your soul and with all your mind… love your neighbour as yourself' (Mt 22: 37 – 40). In practice, however, there is a wide interpretation of morality. For instance, some Christians believe that contraception, abortion, divorce or executions are wrong, while others may not, yet both will use Biblical (and other) arguments to support their position.

The Christian year

There are three main festivals in the Christian year. These are: Easter (resurrection of Jesus from the dead); Christmas (birth of Jesus); and Whitsun or Pentecost (the sending of the Holy Spirit).

In addition, there are many lesser festivals such as saints' and martyrs' days which are celebrated in some churches.

The Church year

Shrove Tuesday – when food is used up and forgiveness is asked before beginning the Lent fast.

Ash Wednesday – when last year's palms are burnt and a mark made on the worshipper's forehead. This day marks the beginning of Lent.

Lent – is the solemn period of 40 days leading up to Easter. It is a reminder of the 40 days Jesus spent in the wilderness. It is a time of reflection and penitence.

Holy Week – the week before Easter begins with Palm Sunday marking Jesus' triumphal entry into Jerusalem; Maundy Thursday remembering the Last Supper, Good Friday – when Jesus was crucified.

Easter Sunday – the most important Christian festival which celebrates the raising of Christ from the dead.

Whitsun or Pentecost – 50 days later. This celebrates the giving of the Holy Spirit, sometimes called the birthday of the Church. Whitsun is a shortening of 'White Sunday', so called because it was traditional for baptisms to be held on this day and those being baptised wore white clothes.

Harvest – thanksgiving for the harvest.

Advent – the four weeks leading up to Christmas. This is a time to prepare for the second coming of Christ.

Christmas – celebrates the birth of Jesus (25 December). Epiphany – associated with the arrival of the three magi (6 January).

Some people think that Christians believe in three Gods. This is a misunderstanding of the doctrine of the Trinity – which states that there is only One God, but that He exists in three different aspects.

Some people also think that different types of churches (denominations) mean a different religion. Although Christians have different understandings of some aspects of how Christianity should be practised, they nevertheless all subscribe to the basic Christian belief in the Trinity.

Christian denominations in the UK

Eastern Orthodox Church
The Eastern Orthodox Church traces its origins to the first disciples of Christ and the early Church.

Catholic
The Roman Catholic Church is the oldest institution in the Western World and the largest Christian denomination. It split from the Eastern Church in 1054 in what is known as the Great Schism. The Pope is head of the Church, whose headquarters are in the Vatican City in Rome.

Church of England
The Church of England is the established or state Church in England. It is part of the Anglican Communion. It was founded in 1534 when Henry VIII broke away from the authority of the Church in Rome.

Church of Scotland
In Scotland the Church became Presbyterian during the Reformation and was made the national Church of Scotland in 1690.

Methodist
The Methodist Church is the fourth largest Christian Church in Britain and belongs to the non-conformist wing of Christianity. Spearheaded by John and Charles Wesley in the 18th century, it grew out of the Anglican Church.

Baptist
Baptists were one of the independent Churches that grew out of the Reformation in the 16th century. Others include the Congregationalists and Presbyterians who joined together in 1972 to form the United Reformed Church. Baptists are the fifth largest denomination in the world. They practise Believers' Baptism.

Quaker
The Quakers (or Religious Society of Friends) are a group with Christian roots that began in England in the 1650s. They are noted for their meetings which do not have a fixed structure but members take part as they feel moved.

Exclusive Brethren
The Exclusive Brethren are an Evangelical Protestant Christian Church related to the Christian or Open Brethren. They do not have television or other modern ITC as they see it as a corrupting influence.

Salvation Army
Founded by William Booth in 1865, as an off-shoot of Methodism, the Salvation Army is well known for its emphasis on helping the poor and deprived. Like the Quakers, they do not practise baptism or communion.

Pentecostalism
Pentecostalism emphasises the Holy Spirit and the experience of God's presence. It grew as a movement in the early 20th century.

Christine Howard

Tell me about God

For many children, pre-school is the first small step into an independent world where they will face new experiences and ask questions. How prepared are you to answer children's questions about God?

In our Christian nursery we aim to expand children's experiences in all areas of life, including spiritual. We do this by talking to them about God as someone who loves them and cares for the world. We share Bible stories and simple thank-you prayers at snack time and the end of each session. We focus on the wonder of nature by looking at flowers, animals and people, acknowledging that God created all of these amazing things.

We also help children learn to respect other people's needs, views, cultures and beliefs and have a policy that satisfies this goal.

We are all used to coping with the constant 'why?' questions that some children like to challenge us with but there are other deeper questions about God and death which are sometimes harder to tackle. Here are a few examples of questions we have had to face and our attempts to answer them.

Who is God?
There are many ways you can answer this.

- God is special. We believe God made this world and all of us.

- We can't know everything about God. The little we can learn about him is from things he made in the world and from the people who love and care for us.

- Look at this flower growing. We can't make it grow. God can do things we can't do.

Children do not need long complicated explanations. They need simple, sincere responses. They will then move on quickly to the next burning question, such as: 'What's for snack?'. It is important to be genuine and if you can't answer a question, say so.

Where do you go when you die?
When children first experience death through the loss of a relative, friend or possibly a pet, they may begin to ask questions about what happens after death. Many faiths believe in heaven or some version of life after death and this can be a comforting idea for a grieving child. There are several helpful story books that tackle this issue in sensitive ways that are suitable for sharing with a pre-school child (see page 39).

Dealing with tragedy
My personal experience of this was tested when a six-year-old boy at our school was tragically killed. This incident sparked off many questions from the children, for example: 'Where is Adam* now?', 'Do you get old in heaven or will he always be six?' Don't be afraid to say 'I don't know'. You can always explain that nobody really knows the answer to some questions but offer your personal belief or thoughts instead.

The school responded in several ways. The class teacher renamed the literacy hour after the child, 'Adam hour', and children were helped to share their memories of their friend in drawing or writing. The teacher asked the children what they wanted to do with all their work. 'Let's put all the pictures in his drawer', suggested one boy. When doing their number work later in the week, one of Adam's group insisted there were still six children in the group and left a chair ready for his missing friend.

A local minister took a special 'goodbye' assembly later that week. He asked the children to picture a large passenger ship waiting to set sail from the docks with lots of people aboard. There was Adam on the ship waving. We all waved goodbye as the ship sailed into the distance, getting smaller and smaller. Even when we could not see the ship or our friend anymore, they were still there, sailing on to heaven.

Where is heaven?
Our response to this question is 'a safe and happy place where you are always with God'. We asked children to tell us their answers to some of these questions. Laura (four) replied, 'Heaven is upstairs at my nursery!' When asked what he thought God was like Bruce (four) drew a picture (illustrated here).

Judith Harries and Ruth Andrews

* The child's name has been changed.

This is a picture of God.
He's got some food in his tummy.
He's very sad because someone's been naughty.
He's got very funny hair and some ears.

Hinduism

The word 'Hindu' comes from the name of an ancient river in India called Sindhu. It was mispronounced 'Hindu' and the people who lived in that part of the country became known as Hindus.

Hinduism is often called a polytheist religion (believing in many gods and goddesses). This is not true. It is a pluralistic religion that suggests that God can be thought of and approached in a variety of ways. This teaching is central to Hinduism. It emphasises that as we are all different, the way we think of the ultimate reality (God) will be different. No religion is better than others.

The 2011 UK census indicates over ¾ million of the population of England and Wales are Hindu. About 70 per cent of them are of Gujarati origin, 15 to 20 per cent are from Punjab and the remainder are from the rest of India.

Basic beliefs

The name given to religious pursuits is dharma. This word can mean 'righteous living'; sometimes it is described as 'the cohesive force that holds society and civilisation together'. The deeper meaning of the word dharma is to search for the innermost nature of everything.

Hinduism offers a vast variety of concepts of God. These can be divided into three main categories. No one approach is better than another, the choice depends on the individual.

God with form and quality:

Hinduism suggests that one of the ways we can relate to the idea of God is to think of Him or Her as having human form (sometimes even superhuman with more than two arms, for example). God can be thought of as a father figure (Vishnu, shown with four arms) or as a mother figure (like Amba, sitting on a tiger or a lion and holding divine weapons). This approach can emphasise certain qualities: the elephant-headed God (Ganesh) brings good luck and the monkey-faced God (Hanuman) depicts strength. The many arms and heads shown on some images of God are there to emphasise their superhuman qualities. The animal faces of some Gods do not mean that Hindus worship animals. When Hindus worship images of God, called murtis (do not make the mistake of calling these images idols, as that is considered demeaning), they are not worshipping the stone or marble that make the images but the being that is represented by those images.

Hindu festivals

Diwali (in the autumn) is perhaps the most popular Hindu festival. It celebrates the return of Rama and Sita from exile, and the day Mother goddess destroyed a demon called Mahisha. On this day people light lamps, visit relations and have feasts and firework displays.

Holi (usually in March) celebrates the arrival of spring.

God without form:

Hinduism also accepts the idea of God without form, represented through concepts like truth, love and power. The worship ceremony adopted in this approach is called Havan. It is carried out by offering grains of fire to build a relationship with God.

Hindus claim that, like ice and water, the same entity can be both with and without form. It is the love of the devotee that freezes the formless God into the form they want. That's why there are so many images of gods and goddesses in Hinduism. They represent tried and tested pathways to God and all these forms are revered.

God beyond form and formless:

The third concept of God says that the inner being we call our self is a manifestation of God. The same God is shining in the eyes of every living thing. The essential nature of all living things is really God. When we help anyone we are helping God. This is why Hinduism teaches reverence for all living things. This definition of God as being our true self is called atman. One of the greetings used by Hindus is 'namaste'. It means literally 'reverence to God as your true self'.

Hindus believe that after we die, we are reborn. This cycle of being born again and again is called reincarnation. Most of us can't remember anything about our past lives but some can. The most important thing that comes with us when we are reborn is our character. That is why children can be born in the same family and have such different characters. We start off as a lower being, like a plant, but slowly evolve and are reborn as higher and higher beings until we become human. It would be difficult to be reborn as a lower being after we have developed a human character. We can stop being reborn after we find God. That is the final destination, called moksha.

Hindus also believe that we have to bear the consequences for all that we do. Sometimes what we do now doesn't catch up with us until later on – in later lives. This is called the Law of Karma. We reap what we sow. It means we have to be careful what we do – if we do hateful things we will have to bear the consequences later. We are responsible for everything that happens to us.

Founders

Hinduism claims many founders, called rishis. The word 'rishi' means 'one who has seen God'. Hinduism claims that the message of spirituality is refreshed in all times and in all countries again and again by seers called rishis.

Scriptures

There is a vast range of scriptures. Some, like the Vedas, tell of the spiritual experiences of the rishis and are considered to have a higher authority. They were written in an ancient language called Sanskrit. Others, like the mythological stories, are called the Puranas and are less important. The **Bhagavad Gita** is considered by most Hindus to be the most authoritative scripture in their religion. It is Krishna's explanation of the philosophy of Hinduism and how it can be adopted in daily life.

Hindu children at school

Hindu children find it easy to mix with children from other faiths and normally Hindu parents will not insist that their children do not participate in any sessions where other religions are being explained. Taking part in music, dance, art, drama or PE poses no special problems. There are no special dress codes or restrictions on clothing.

Diet

Many Hindu children who come from Gujarat or from Tamil-Nadu may be vegetarian. This means that they do not eat meat, fish or eggs. However, cakes or biscuits containing eggs are generally considered acceptable. Nowadays quite a few Hindu families living in the UK (including some families from Gujarat and Tamil-Nadu) have adopted meat-eating habits. The only meat they will not eat is beef as the cow is considered to be the most sacred animal.

Sectarian movements

Hinduism is represented in the UK by many sectarian bodies. There is a great difference in the way they perceive and approach God and this can cause confusion.

The main sectarian bodies in the UK are the Swaminarayan movement, which believes in God with form and quality (as Lord Narayan or Vishnu) and the ISKCON (the Hare Krishna movement), which also promotes the idea of God with form and quality but places greater emphasis on Krishna as the main incarnation of Vishnu. There are other sectarian bodies that place emphasis on God as the mother (Shakti) or God as Shiva (Shiva devotees are called Shaivaits). All these sectarian bodies co-exist within Hinduism and are all considered to represent valid Hindu pathways to God.

Worship

Hinduism teaches that heartfelt love for God counts more than any strict formal codes or rituals. Any activity which takes us closer to God is called worship. Hence the rules of worship or prayers can vary a great deal from family to family. The prayer that all Hindus consider to be central is called the Gayatri.

The Hindu place of worship is a mandir or a temple. There are no hard and fast rules about when to go, but the best time is thought to be dusk or dawn. Hindus may take fruit or flowers as offerings. When they arrive, they take off their shoes before entering. There is normally a bell to ring to announce your presence to God. The main deity (form of God being worshipped) is normally kept in the inner shrine. The outer walls may have smaller shrines showing other deities. There may be singing (bhajans) accompanied by musical instruments. They may observe the aarti ceremony, where a lamp is gently waved in front of the deity in a clockwise direction. The lamp is passed around and everyone cups their hands over it to receive blessings. They may go round the image to pay their respects. When they leave, they are given prashad (the food that was offered during worship).

Yoga

The word 'yoga' is often associated with postures and physical exercises but it has a deeper meaning. It means 'pathway of communing with God through meditation'. Practising short periods of silence or contemplation (without reference to any religion or God) may be a good way to introduce meditation to your group.

Jay Lakhani, Vivekananda Centre, London, a non-commercial non-sectarian body involved in Hindu educational activities.

Teachings of Hinduism

The sanctity of life: The principle of non-violence, called Ahimsa, is central to Hindu teachings. It teaches respect for living things – animals and plants.

Yoga: Practised as a pause before starting any activity, can be a good tool to introduce the idea of self-discipline.

Tolerance: Hindus believe that people from many religions can live together even though they all have different notions of God and practise different approaches to God – all methods can be equally valid.

Humanism

Non-religious people are a growing section of the British population – the 2011 census indicated 25% of the population of England and Wales have no religion. Of these 15,067 identify themselves as humanists.

Humanism has a long and multicultural history stretching back to the ancient Greeks and beyond, but it was only in the last two centuries that humanist thinking became mainstream in Europe and the West, that humanist organisations were formed and the word 'humanist' acquired its modern meaning.

Basic beliefs

There are probably almost as many definitions of humanism as there are humanists, but the one currently used by the British Humanist Association is:

'Humanism is the belief that we can live good lives without religious or superstitious beliefs. Humanists make sense of the world using reason, experience and shared human values. We seek to make the best of the one life we have by creating meaning and purpose for ourselves. We take responsibility for our own actions and work with others for the common good.'

Humanist moral values are likely to be similar to those of most of the world's faiths. Reason and experience lead us to avoid, for example, dishonesty and hurting others; they teach us that life goes better if we respect others and behave kindly and cooperatively.

Where humanism differs from religions is in the absence of any belief in the supernatural – God, the soul, the afterlife, ghosts, miracles – and hence the absence of supernatural influences on our lives or behaviour. The positive aspects of humanism are based on ideas of personal responsibility, and the belief that our moral values stem from ourselves and our needs, not from authority or tradition or revelation. We believe that making things go well is up to us, and the rewards for behaving well are here and now, in personal relationships and the happiness of oneself and others.

What does this mean for you?

Religious education is firmly embedded in the Foundation Stage curriculum and likely to stay there. What can this mean for the many children who arrive at nursery or school with no family connection to a religion and few, if any, family religious beliefs?

Young children from non-religious families must sometimes feel puzzled by all the religion they meet at school, so unlike life and values at home, but humanist and other non-religious parents rarely object to their children learning about other beliefs. They acknowledge that a wide spectrum of beliefs and the stories and traditions of the world's religions are interesting and part of contemporary culture, and they want their children to understand diversity.

They may, however, object to their children being taught that these beliefs or stories are true, or that the beliefs of the six main world faiths are the only possible ideas about the nature of the world and humanity.

To accommodate the occasional parents who want to exercise their right to excuse their child from RE, it is helpful to keep RE separate from other activities such as art, though this may not be easy in the pre-school context.

Understanding there are reasons

Many humanist parents would be happier if their own beliefs were acknowledged and taught about, as well as those of the world religions. Many practitioners will be more than half-way there already. For what most humanist parents want is not abstract discussions about the existence of God or the soul but the use of reason, and reasons, when talking about moral values and behaviour.

Humanists believe that there are good everyday (non-religious) reasons for trying to be good. Whenever you say to a child: 'How would you like it if your friend did that to you?' or 'What would this place be like if everyone did that?' or 'You're making me / your mummy very sad by doing that', you are using good human(ist) reasons. Others might include: 'Isn't life better when people are nice/kind to you/ each other?'; 'Do you really want to be the sort of person who …?'; 'Is that fair?'.

Personal values

Whenever you use this kind of reasoning, you are teaching children to empathise and to think about the consequences of their choices and actions, and reinforcing their intuitions about justice. Stories from all kinds of traditions, religious and secular, circle time, games and cooperative activities, can also support the development of personal skills and attitudes, as well as the thoughtful and mutually respectful discussion of ideas and values that is an ideal of humanism.

Humanist parents will also hope for their children to learn there are others like them. You do not have to go into philosophy to teach that there are people who do not believe in God or the power of prayer, or who appreciate the beauty of the universe without believing that it was created, who believe that good lives and behaviour can be based on reason and experience – and why they hold these beliefs. When a child talks about a baby or a wedding in the family, the class can learn about humanist ways of celebrating these happy events, as well as religious ones.

Death and funerals

When deaths occur in your community and need to be talked over, humanist parents prefer an acknowledgment that for some people death is the end and that not everyone believes in life after death or heaven. Humanists try to remember and be grateful for the good things and the happy memories left behind by the person they have lost. There are many books for young children exploring death in these terms.

Most humanist objections can be dealt with quite simply by slight shifts in language or emphasis, saying: 'Some people believe…'; 'Some Christians do…'; 'This is a story that Muslims believe'; 'This is how … think the world began'. Otherwise humanist parents may feel obliged to say what I did when my children brought these ideas home: 'Some people believe that, but I don't'. We don't want to undermine the developing trust between children and their teachers, but neither do we want our beliefs to be undermined or our children misled.

Worship and prayer

Although humanists and other atheists do not worship or pray, they rarely exercise their right to remove their children from school worship. Most of them want their children to experience this sharing of values and news, and don't want them to be singled out as odd. There are ways to make them feel included, for example by taking stories from a range of cultures, including secular ones, and allowing children to pray or reflect.

Humanists, like everyone else, have hopes for the world and ideas they can reflect on quietly, and they don't mind others praying around them. There are plenty of songs for assemblies that celebrate the world and encourage children to be caring and thoughtful without invoking religion.

Attitudes to Nativity plays and other religious festivities vary, but most humanist parents welcome efforts to include their children without assuming or demanding belief.

Nurseries or playgroups in church halls can be problematical for some humanist parents if they are too closely identified with the church. Ideally, the group would have a separate identity from the building it is in, and would not be named after the church or display religious posters or artefacts. Resources generally should be carefully selected, to avoid religious indoctrination or offence.

Many pre-schools already practise humanist values and methods, perhaps without being conscious of it. To make them more explicit by, for example, occasionally talking about moral reasoning or using the word 'humanist' would not be hard. It would provide some children with an introduction to a world view that might mean much to them later, while others would begin to understand beliefs that they will encounter as they grow up.

Marilyn Mason, British Humanist Association

Useful addresses and websites

- British Humanist Association (BHA) 39, Moreland Street, London EC1V 8BB. Tel: 020 7324 3060 or email: education@humanism.org.uk
- See www.humanism.org.uk for more education resources/useful ideas and materials.

Islam

* When Muslims speak or write the name of Muhammad they always add the phrase 'Peace be upon him' afterwards. ** Common Era – term used by Jews and Muslims instead of the Christian Anno Domini.

The 2011 census indicates over 2.7 million of the population of England and Wales are Muslim.

Islam is the religion and way of life that teaches wholehearted acceptance of guidance from Allah, the Arabic word for 'the one and only true God'. Those who follow this religion are called Muslims. The Arabic word islam means the acceptance of, and obedience to, the guiding wisdom of Allah.

Islam came into being with the revelation of the Qur'an (Koran) to the Prophet Muhammad (Peace be upon him*) in 610 to 632 CE**, which makes it more than 1,400 years old. The message of the Qur'an spread rapidly through the Middle East, North Africa and South Asia, but Muslims are now found in many different parts of the world.

Basic beliefs

Muslims believe that there is only one God, the same God worshipped by Christians and Jews, whose main name is **Allah**. He also has many attributes (also called 'names') mentioned in the **Qur'an**, the Muslim holy book.

Muslims believe that the Qur'an was revealed by Allah to the Prophet Muhammad and that he memorised it and had it written down so that it still contains exactly the same words, in Arabic, that were revealed to him.

They believe that the Qur'an is the last of the messages to human beings that Allah revealed via His many prophets and messengers. These are not only the ones mentioned in the Bible, including Jesus, but also some Arab prophets, and a large number of other messengers sent to all other peoples.

Islamic teachings

The Qur'an teaches that God wants people to be good, kind and patient, to return good for evil, and never to lose hope of His mercy. It promotes sharing, through zakah (charitable giving), cleanliness, discipline and consciousness of God (through prayer), self-restraint through fasting and many other virtues.

According to the Qur'an, just as Allah made fruits and rocks of different colours, so He made human beings of different colours. We are all children of Adam and Eve and those most honoured in the sight of Allah are those who are most aware of Him. On the Hajj or pilgrimage to Makkah (Mecca) Muslims of all races come together from all over the world to worship God.

The Qur'an teaches people to stand up for justice, to protect the weak and vulnerable, and allows fighting in self-defence. But it also tells people to stop fighting as soon as the enemy ceases to attack. It teaches people that if their enemy wants to make peace they should agree to it, and keep their promises, providing their enemies keep theirs. It also tells people to make peace between others who are fighting.

Muslim children at school

Art
Islam forbids the worship of idols, and so many Muslims avoid representing human or animal figures.

Music
In Islam the only music which is universally accepted by all Muslims is the recitation of the Holy Qur'an. Many Muslims avoid music, and may not wish their children to join in music sessions. However, you should discuss this issue with Muslim parents as often what is actually abhorrent is the idea of pop or disco music; religious songs (nasheeds), folk or appropriate cultural music may be acceptable.

Young children may be allowed to take part in music and movement sessions which aim to sensitise them to the natural world, for example blowing like a leaf in the wind.

Dance
Some Muslims may accept folk and cultural dances taught to single-sex groups. The more expressive forms of dance, such as ballet, are likely to be less welcomed or understood. The clothes pupils wear for dance must be modest, loose and fully covering. Leotards are not suitable, nor are vests and pants.

PE
Muslim children can do PE in mixed classes up to the age of puberty but should dress modestly. (Single-sex schools are preferred for children after they reach the age of puberty.)

Drama
Muslim parents would prefer their children not to take part in Nativity plays, act the parts of Hindu deities, or animals such as dogs or pigs, for example. Role play is not likely to be problematic. Those areas unacceptable in Islam are public performance, physical contact between mixed players and role swapping (girls dressing as boys and vice versa).

Dress requirements
Islamic dress for both sexes should be modest and not

tight fitting, transparent or accentuating the body shape. In practice, this means a wide variety of styles can be worn. Boys should always be covered between the navel and knee and girls reveal only their hands, feet and faces.

Many Muslim children wear Qur'anic verses, which may be wrapped or sewn in cloth or contained in small metal boxes or lockets worn on a chain or string around the neck or upper arm, or pinned inside clothes. These are religious artefacts and not jewellery. It would display great understanding if pupils were not required to remove them.

Diet

Muslims are only allowed to eat meat if is halal, which means 'by law/allowed' and has had God's name pronounced over it in the prescribed manner. Muslims do not eat sausages, bacon, pork, ham or any other form of meat by-product, including gelatine, which originates from the pig. Nor is any food cooked in fat or lard from pig products, including cheeses made with animal rennet. (Pig meat is considered filthy by Muslims and some may take offence at stories and pictures about pigs.) Halal meat is suitable for most non-Muslim children to eat and can be made into burgers or any other dish.

Muslims always use their right hand to convey food from the plate to their mouth. Some eat with their fingers, while others use cutlery, held in the right hand. Foods that need cutting will be eaten with the right hand after being sliced.

Cleanliness

Each time a Muslim has used the toilet, running water is used and the private parts are thoroughly washed using the cleaned left hand. The child sits on the toilet and the clean water is poured over the private parts from a jug or bottle held in the right hand so that all the water goes into the toilet to be flushed away. (It would be useful to provide plastic jugs or small watering cans in the toilets for this purpose.)

Muslims pray five times daily and no prayer is acceptable unless the person is in a state of purity, which is symbolised by the washing of hands, faces, head and feet (wudu).

Salah – prayer

Young Muslim children are encouraged to learn the Islamic prayer by imitating their elders, and are taught to memorise short sections (suras) of the Qur'an, although they do not have to pray regularly until they are ten years old. Most children at nursery would not need to do their prayers at school, unless their school day is very long. However, they may have learned short Arabic prayers (du'a) to recite before such actions as eating and sleeping and should be encouraged to continue this practice.

The place for communal Muslim worship is called a mosque. Muslims are required to pray five times a day, and although this need not be at a mosque, it must be done according to precisely laid down rules.

Sawm – Fasting

During the lunar month of Ramadan, many Muslim children will fast for some or all of the 29 to 30 days of that month. Children may start to fast from any age they feel able to do so. This is often undertaken progressively over the years – up to lunchtime for the first year, the following year till teatime – until by puberty most practising Muslim children will fast from dawn to sunset. Young children are encouraged to do whatever they can, for example go without crisps or sweets. Fasting not only involves abstaining from food, but from liquid too, including water.

People who are fasting must take particular care to refrain from petty wrongdoings or giving way to ill temper during this month.

Anything that is not food or drink does not break the fast. However, some Muslims consider nose and eye drops that may enter the throat to break the fast, so it is always good practice to consult parents on these matters as interpretation, as well as the level of personal commitment, may vary.

Eid – religious holidays

Days on which Muslim pupils will almost certainly ask for permission to be absent are: Eid ul-Fitr – the day which celebrates the end of the fasting month of Ramadan, and Eid ul-Adha – the day that celebrates the end of the Hajj (pilgrimage to Makkah). On both these days Muslims attend the mosque early in the morning for prayers. The rest of the day is spent visiting friends and relatives.

All information supplied by IQRA Trust.

The five basic duties (pillars) of Islam

- **Shahadah** – declaration of faith
- **Salah** – five obligatory daily prayers
- **Zakah** – welfare due
- **Sawm** – fasting during Ramadan
- **Hajj** – pilgrimage to Makkah.

Useful addresses

- IQRA Trust (www.iqratrust.com) aims to provide clear, accurate and reliable information about the faith of Islam and the Muslim way of life. The trust works with LAs, schools and teachers.
- The Muslim Educational Trust, 130 Stroud Green Road, London, N4 3RZ. Tel: 0207 272 8502. Publishes a range of books including *Islam: Beliefs and Teachings* by Ghulam Sarwar and a free leaflet called *Islam – a Brief Guide* (please send a SAE).

Jehovah's Witnesses

The movement that became the Jehovah's Witnesses began in the early 1870s in Pittsburgh, Pennsylvania, with Bible study classes involving people from various Christian backgrounds. It was known at first as the Russellite movement or the Bible Students but eventually Jehovah's Witnesses became the name accepted worldwide.

In the 1880s there were scores of congregations in nearby states and the magazine, later to be called The Watchtower, was used to help in the weekly Bible class discussion. Publication and distribution of Bible literature is seen as fulfilling the commission of Jesus to preach to all the world and has remained a major objective to the present day. By 1909 the headquarters had moved to New York. The first representatives were sent to Britain in 1881 with a London branch opened in 1900.

Today there are more than 6 million Jehovah's Witnesses around the world; around 130,000 in the UK.

Core beliefs

- Jehovah's Witnesses believe that God created the earth and will preserve it. Jehovah is God's personal name which occurs more than 7,000 times in the Bible.

- Jehovah's Witnesses place themselves today as a continuation of a long line of Witnesses for God that started with Abel, the son of Adam and Eve.

- They believe that the Bible is the Word of God, divinely inspired and historically accurate. They prefer to use their own *New World Translation of the Holy Scriptures*, first published in 1961.

- Jehovah's Witnesses believe that Jesus is the Son of God and Chief Witness; they reject the doctrine of the Trinity. They believe that Jesus is God's only direct creation, that all other creation was through him and that he suffered a sacrificial death. They believe that Christ came to rule in Kingdom Power in the heavens in 1914.

- They believe that Satan is an active force and that is why there are so many problems in the world today. Soon, at the Battle of Armageddon, Jesus will extend God's Kingdom rule to include the whole earth. Jehovah's Witnesses attempt to lead blameless lives in preparation for the millennial rule of Christ. They recognise that their salvation is not by works but rather by Jehovah God's undeserved kindness 'through Christ Jesus'.

- The family is seen as the cornerstone of the God-ruled society. The father is recognised as the head of the family just as Christ is the head of humankind. Male leadership is recognised within the congregation; women also have a vital role to play.

- The place of worship is called a Kingdom Hall and members are encouraged to be active propagators of the faith, which includes the distribution of literature. Children of Witnesses are encouraged to serve and make a personal commitment before qualifying for baptism which is by total immersion. Baptism takes place after a person has taken in knowledge of God's Word and can make an intelligent decision.

- The Memorial Celebration is the most important event of the year for Jehovah's Witnesses. It commemorates the death of Jesus and follows the pattern commanded by Jesus at his Last Supper with his faithful companions. Jehovah's Witnesses observe the memorial on Nisan 14 which is carefully reckoned from the first century Jewish calendar (it is usually in March or April but falls on a different date each year). This special day lasts from sundown on Nisan 14 to the next sundown.

Advice and good practice

If you have children within your group from families which are Jehovah's Witnesses you need to be conscious of their distinctive religious position; their parents will hold opinions on several issues which are relevant to their children's education. You should make every effort to affirm their place in the community, avoiding any potential embarrassment that might be caused by the requirements of their faith.

Jehovah's Witnesses recognise the right of others to hold their own views and practices and so you should respond with the same degree of respect towards them. If you are uncertain about anything concerning Jehovah's Witness children, contact their parents at an early stage so that possible misunderstandings can be avoided.

The Watchtower Bible and Tract Society makes the following statement in *Jehovah's Witnesses and Education* (page 29): 'Jehovah's Witnesses feel that their children are better served when parents cooperate with educators taking an active, helpful interest in their children's education'.

Religious education

Jehovah's Witnesses believe that religious education is the responsibility of the parents. Parents have the legal right to withdraw their child from religious education. On this issue in particular prior consultation with parents is more important on the content of the lessons to be taught. Following discussion with the setting or school Jehovah's Witness parents might agree for their children to be present in some of the lessons.

Collective worship

Jehovah's Witnesses have no objection to their children attending a general school assembly as long as it is not for the purpose of 'collective worship'. They will exercise their legal right to withdraw their children. It might be helpful where a significant number of Jehovah's Witness children are withdrawn from collective worship for an alternative activity to be planned, perhaps with the help of their parents.

Citizenship

Jehovah's Witnesses believe that all honours should be paid only to God so they do not salute a national flag or stand during the national anthem. Neither do they take part in political activities.

During the two world wars many Jehovah's Witnesses were imprisoned because of their belief in Christian neutrality. They were persecuted because of this during the 1930s and 1940s, particularly for their refusal to participate in armed warfare or the giving of allegiance to national symbols, such as a flag. They do not take part in Remembrance events of the wars.

Charitable activities

Jehovah's Witness parents may be willing to allow their children to take part in general charitable activities. However, they would not want them to participate in religious based charities or any involved in the remembrance of war – they would never wear the red poppy. If there is any uncertainty, always check with parents.

Festivals

When lessons are about the festivals of world faiths, Jehovah's Witness parents would not want their children to be involved. For example, Jehovah's Witnesses do not celebrate Christmas and Easter, believing that there is no scriptural justification for them and that they are rooted in paganism. Many of the key activities which might take place such as a Nativity play, making Christmas cards or decorating Christmas trees would be unacceptable. Painting a snow scene as an alternative in these circumstances would be acceptable. There are also objections to the symbol of the cross as Jehovah's Witnesses believe that Jesus was nailed to a tree. However, if references to these festivals are incidental, such as in an art lesson, Jehovah's Witness parents would probably not be too concerned.

'Children of Jehovah's Witnesses are taught to be tolerant and respectful, and this includes recognising the right of others to celebrate Christmas. In turn, they appreciate it when their decision not to participate in Christmas celebrations is respected.' (*Jehovah's Witnesses and Education* 1995, page 18.)

Birthdays

Jehovah's Witnesses do not recognise secular anniversaries such as birthdays and Mother's Day or Father's Day. They would not want their children to participate in birthday celebrations, such as singing 'Happy birthday'.

They would also be likely to object if stories were used which advocated the celebrating of birthdays. However, you should not become anxious that Jehovah's Witness parents would be concerned about incidental references to such occasions in the normal course of pre-school life.

Medical issues

Jehovah's Witnesses refuse blood transfusions on scriptural grounds and also believe that there are inherent medical dangers in the procedure. An Identity and Advance Medical Directive/Release card is carried by Witnesses in case of emergency. Jehovah's Witness children should have such a card in their possession at all times which also bears the names of two people to be contacted in the event of a medical emergency. Hospitals are aware of the existence of such cards. It is a good idea to ask for a copy of the card to keep in the child's file.

Based on information supplied by the Watch Tower Bible and Tract Society of Britain.

Useful addresses

- To consult Jehovah's Witnesses on issues relating to their beliefs contact: Watch Tower Bible and Tract Society of Britain, The Ridgeway, London, NW7 1RN. Tel: 020 8906 2211.
- The Jehovah's Witness official website: www.jw.org
- Further understanding on matters relating to minority religious groups in general can be sought from: Information Network Focus on Religious Movements (INFORM), Houghton Street, London, WC2A 2AE. Tel: 020 7955 7654.

Judaism

The founder of Judaism was Abraham, whose custom of hospitality and strong acknowledgement of God's unity and power still form the foundations of Jewish practice today. Abraham lived about 4,000 years ago and his life is described in the Biblical book of Genesis.

Judaism is based on the Torah, the Hebrew term for the Five Books of Moses. The Torah is written in Hebrew. Jews pray in Hebrew and many of the terms that follow are in that language.

Basic beliefs

Orthodox Jews believe that the **Torah** is a complete guide to everyday life. As every generation throws up different perspectives on old problems, there is a constant flow of questions and answers to guide Jewish people in keeping the Torah in today's world. Rabbis with a deep understanding of sacred texts keep the traditions alive through this dialogue.

Jews believe in one God and in the mitzvot or commandments that it is their duty to fulfil in order to obey His will. The Ten Commandments revealed on Mount Sinai form the basic guide to Jewish behaviour.

These sum up the two major categories into which Jewish Laws are divided – relationships with the Almighty and relationships with human beings.

There is respect for the religion and customs of countries in which Jews live. Jews do not try to convert others to their faith and they have a positive duty to care for other people especially the weak and vulnerable of any faith or none.

Worship and prayer

The synagogue is where communal Jewish prayer takes place, but many other prayer activities take place in the home. Jews should pray three times each day, with extra prayers on Sabbaths and holy days. The synagogue also often acts as a community centre, with activities which could range from mother and toddler groups to senior citizen discussion circles.

The Sabbath

Shabbat, the Jewish Sabbath, lasts from sunset on Friday until sunset on Saturday. As these times change with the seasons it means that the Sabbath starts early on winter afternoons.

During the Sabbath, Orthodox Jews do not travel in a vehicle, cook, use electricity or write, amongst other things, to enable a complete cessation of weekday work activities. Any child in your care would need to reach home before the onset of the Sabbath. These times can be found in the weekly publication *The Jewish Chronicle* (or at their website: www.thejc.com).

The start of the Sabbath on Friday is accompanied by a candle-lighting ceremony. The Shabbat meal includes the traditional two plaited loaves, called challot (ch as in 'loch'). These represent the two portions of manna collected by the Israelites in the wilderness on the sixth day.

One of the main features of the Sabbath synagogue service is the reading of the Law. The Five Books of Moses (called the Torah, Law in Hebrew) are divided into 54 sections and the whole cycle is read aloud in the course of a year. The Sabbath ends with a ceremony called Havdalah which means 'separation' (between Sabbath and the rest of the week).

The Jewish calendar

There is a Jewish calendar with months which coincide with the new moon (a lunar calendar). The festivals are at fixed dates in the Jewish calendar but may vary from year to year in the regular (solar) calendar. Festivals remain roughly in their season, for example Passover must always be in springtime.

The year begins in the autumn with the Solemn Days of the New Year and the Day of Atonement.

There are many festivals during the autumn, concentrated into a month, usually September/October. Children may be absent from school for up to seven days, depending on when the festivals occur. This can be disruptive so early in the school year but the timing is not negotiable – neither rabbis nor anyone in authority have the power to change them.

Food

Kosher is the term applied to food products that comply with Jewish dietary laws. *The Really Jewish Food Guide* gives a comprehensive listing of kosher products (copies are available from www.kosher.org.uk – this website also contains general information on Jewish dietary laws).

Meat products must be produced under rabbinical supervision. Other foods that need a kosher certification are all processed foods, for example biscuits and cheese. Even vegetarian foods may contain non-kosher ingredients in food additives.

Festivals

Rosh Hashanah (September) – Jewish New Year. This lasts for two days when children will stay at home to celebrate with their families. The *shofar*, a ram's horn, is blown in synagogue as a call to repentance. Among the food customs associated with this festival are the eating of sweet foods, for example apple dipped in honey, honey cake, symbolising a sweet new year, and the replacement of the traditional plaited *challot* by round ones, symbolising the cycle of the year.

Yom Kippur (September) – Day of Atonement. A day of fasting and prayer for forgiveness. Children are not expected to fast. Girls reach the age of responsibility to fast at the age of 12, boys at the age of 13. Younger children may opt to fast for part of the day. They will not come to school on Yom Kippur.

Sukkot (September/October) – Tabernacles, the Jewish harvest festival. Huts or tabernacles (*Succot* in Hebrew) are built, with flat roofs made of leaves or natural materials. It is traditional to invite many guests. The *succah* is often decorated with fruits as a symbol of the harvest; it also symbolises the fragility of human beings who depend for their safety not just on their own efforts but on the protection of the Almighty. The festival lasts for eight days and children may come to school on the intermediate days (third to seventh day inclusive).

Simchat Torah (September/October) – Rejoicing in the Law. A day to celebrate the completion of the reading of one cycle of the *Law*, the Five Books of Moses, and the beginning of a new cycle. It occurs immediately after Sukkot.

Hanukkah (December/January) – An eight-day festival when lights are kindled every evening to commemorate the rededication of the Temple in 165 BCE (Before Common Era – term used by Jews and Muslims instead of Before Christ), after the oppression and desecration by the Greek ruler of Judea, Antiochus Epiphanes. This is a family time and children enjoy playing traditional games, although it is a normal work day.

Purim (February/March) A day of commemoration of the victory of Queen Esther over the wicked Haman, a Persian minister who hated Jews and was hanged for plotting to massacre them. It is celebrated by fancy dress, a special meal, and the giving of gifts to neighbours and to the poor.

There are about 300,000 Jews in Britain. They live in all parts of the country from Aberdeen to Cornwall and from Belfast to Norwich. However, historically they have congregated in particular areas because of the sense of support that comes from living as part of a community. Among the most well-known areas in the past were the east end of London, Cheetham Hill in Manchester and Chapeltown in Leeds. The main centre of Jewish population is Greater London.

Pesach (March/April) – Passover. A week-long festival to remember the exodus from Egypt of the Hebrew slaves. The Biblical story of Exodus is re-enacted in a family celebration at home called a *seder*. A *seder* service is held on the first two nights of Passover for Jews who live outside Israel.

The most well-known feature of this festival is the eating of unleavened bread, matzah, and the absence of bread. No leavened food (containing yeast) may be eaten. Children may be in school from the third to the sixth days of the festival; Passover often coincides with Easter and there may be school holidays.

Shavuot (May/June) – Pentecost. This festival celebrates the giving of the Ten Commandments on Mount Sinai. The Ten Commandments are read aloud in synagogues, which are decorated with flowers. It is traditional to study the Torah all night; the traditional food is cheesecake.

Symbols

Sefer Torah – Book of the Law
The book of the Law is a handwritten scroll containing the Hebrew of the Five Books of Moses. The text has been fixed for 2,000 years. It is treasured not only for its content but also for the precise detailed hand work involved in preparing it. It is covered with a decorated mantle and kept in a specially designed cupboard in the front of the synagogue.

Mezuzah – Doorpost scroll
The mezuzah contains short handwritten sections from the Five Books of Moses. It is fixed to the upper right doorpost of every room in a Jewish home, school or building, except the toilet.

Tallit – Prayer shawl
Men wear a prayer shawl for the morning service. It has four knotted fringes on its corners, which are a constant reminder to the wearer of the connection to the Torah and its mitzvot.

At pre-school and school
Assembly: Jewish children may wish to be excluded from prayers and will not recite the Lord's Prayer.

Drama: Jewish children may not want to participate in Nativity plays.

Dress: Orthodox Jewish boys wear a skullcap (kippah or capel) and tzitzit, which is a garment with fringed corners worn under the shirt.

Food: Where food is shared, for example for a party or celebration, orthodox Jewish children will only eat kosher food. When in doubt, provide fresh fruit or vegetables.

Information supplied by the Agency for Jewish Education.

Religious Society of Friends (Quakers)

There are about 25,000 people involved with Quakerism in Britain. They have a special view of what religion means, and of Christianity in particular.

Quakerism started in England in the 1640s, during the Civil War, with a man called George Fox. He went around the country trying to find a form of religious belief that made sense to him.

On his travels, he met many other people like him who looked to the early days of the Christian church for inspiration. They felt that over the centuries the church had led people away from the real aims of Christianity and become preoccupied with traditions, rituals and the politics of power.

Fox and his followers were often imprisoned for their honesty and refusal to compromise. In 1689 they were granted some measure of tolerance and after that they were persecuted less. They lost some of their zeal and became more inward looking, but even though these Quakers, as they were now known, withdrew from the world they remained idealistic. They still preached a message of equality, justice, peace and simplicity.

These early Quakers were trying to lead a renewal – to see how they could live life more simply and truthfully, following Jesus' example more closely. There's no doubt that Quakerism is rooted in Christianity and many Quakers centre their faith on Jesus. However, some find that traditional religious language doesn't describe their inner experiences and they look both within Christianity and beyond.

Quakers recognise all the great faiths as ways to spiritual fulfilment and they are willing to learn from and work with other faiths and churches.

What do Quakers believe?

Quakers have no set creed or dogma – that means they don't have any declared statement which you have to believe to be a Quaker. What is important for Quakers is not what you say you believe but how you live your everyday life.

The name Quaker started as a nickname – their real name is the Religious Society of Friends but they are happy to be called either Friends or Quakers.

However, there are some commonly held views which unite them. One view is that there is something of God in all people and that every human being is of unique worth. Quakers therefore try to value all people and not to harm or threaten them.

Quakers have many beliefs and attitudes in common, but you can't list them or use them as a test of membership. Friends talk of an 'inward light' within every human being. Some would call this 'conscience' or 'moral sense' but Friends feel it is something more: part of spiritual and religious experience, which gives you a sense of direction in your search for the right way to live.

Friends have always questioned anything they were told to believe. This is part of their 'seeking for truth'. It is based on the belief that there is a direct relationship between each person and God.

Quakers don't spend much time discussing theology, for example whether Jesus was the son of God. They would say the important thing is to learn from Jesus' teaching and way of life.

In Britain, most Friends see the Bible as the greatest printed source of inspiration, but not the only one. They value it, for example as a record of the struggle of a people to establish a society based on justice, righteousness and love. They don't see it as the word of God and they don't think everything in the Bible is relevant today, for example slavery was taken for granted in Biblical times and the social role of women has changed.

Meeting for worship

The word 'meeting' means several different things to Quakers. It can mean the place people worship in, the group of people worshipping together and it can refer to the act of worship itself.

The meeting house is not like a church. There are no statues, altar or pulpit. Chairs are arranged in a circle or around a table on which there may be some flowers and books, usually the Bible.

The meeting begins when the first person sits down in silence. There may be more than a hundred people or just five or six. Many meetings have children's groups. Sometimes the children will stay for the first quarter of an hour, sometimes they will be there for the last quarter. When they go out they will have their own activities depending on their age and number.

Some meetings sit in complete silence for the hour, but it is more usual for there to be two or three spoken contributions which are known as vocal ministry. These may be readings from the Bible or other books or something the speaker has experienced or thought about. Speaking is not taken lightly in a Quaker meeting. The speaker will feel moved and inspired to speak and the contribution should be spontaneous.

According to one story, early Friends got the nickname 'Quaker' because they were so moved in their worship that they sometimes quaked or shook. Another story has it that George Fox told a judge that he ought to tremble before God's judgement and that the judge called Fox a Quaker or trembler.

In the meeting for worship, Friends share with each other what they have found out for themselves, and gain from each other in this way. Some Quakers may be praying inwardly, others thinking of the people who need their help, reflecting about their lives and where they need forgiveness or need to forgive. There is no priest, no hymns, no sermon, no taking of bread and wine. It is a communion based on silence. After about an hour the elders, who are responsible for running the meeting, will shake hands as a sign that the meeting is over. After notices read by the clerk, coffee or tea may be served and newcomers welcomed.

Anybody can go to a local Quaker meeting for worship. If they find they share Friends' outlook, they can become a member.

Lifestyle

Quakers feel that it's no good having a faith unless you put it into practice. So they have always tried to be honest at work. They try to live a fairly simple life and not get too worried about money, possessions or status, nor to lose sight of what is really important.

They aim for truthfulness at all times, which is why, for example, a Quaker won't swear an oath in court – it would suggest that the rest of the time you can have different standards of truth.

Quakers have always felt strongly about improving social conditions and the environment. Help for slaves, prisoners,

mental patients, refugees, old people, war casualties – quite a few charities and campaigns for reform have started as the concern of a Quaker. Some of Britain's greatest social reformers, such as Elizabeth Fry, were Quakers. So, too, were leading industrialists like the Cadbury and Rowntree families, much of whose money went into financing social projects.

Quakers say that if you follow the teaching and life of Jesus, you must rule out wars and violence as a way of solving problems. So Friends have always worked for peace, refusing to join in wars and military action. On a national level they work to bring together diplomats from different and often rival countries. You will also find Quakers in counselling and law centres or on the high street, holding vigils or demonstrating for a safer world.

They believe that peace is not just the absence of war but about relationships with families and neighbours. It's about how we cope with people we may find difficult and different from ourselves.

War play

One of the main things you need to know about if you work with children from Quaker families is their attitude to violence and war. It is safe to say that all Quakers are concerned with building a more peaceful world where conflicts are dealt with in non-violent ways, whether at a personal, local, national or international level. Conflict, disagreements and differences of opinion are seen as a natural part of daily life and not bad in itself; it is how people respond to conflict that concerns Quakers.

Quakers are generally liberal in outlook and would be loathe to ban anything, such as toy guns. They accept that children will act out what they have seen, perhaps on television, and so would advise practitioners to use their judgment with individual cases. What they would encourage is for settings to have a policy on conflict resolution, so that everyone knows how to deal with a situation when it arises and children learn to work out their problems in a non-violent way.

Based on information supplied by the Religious Society of Friends.

Festivals

Friends believe that if there is something of God in every person – and every time and place and thing – then there is no need for special feast days, ceremonies and sacraments such as baptism or holy communion. In the same way, the Friends' meeting house is not a consecrated building; it can just as well be used for music, eating, discussion or fun as for worship. For Quakers, there should be no split between religion and daily life.

Seventh-day Adventists

Seventh-day Adventists did not set out to be a separate denomination. Founder members came from various denominations and met for Bible study and Christian fellowship. They were Methodist, Baptist and Anglican people, and members of all kinds of European churches who held one compelling belief in common – they all believed that Jesus was coming soon.

They met informally for 20 years in the mid 1800s before they decided to organise officially into a denomination in 1863. By the year 2000 worldwide membership of the Seventh-day Adventist Church was nearly 12 million.

Adventists in the UK

The first Seventh-day Adventist Church in the UK was established in 1886. The British Union Conference of Seventh-day Adventists was officially organised in 1902 and its headquarters is based at Stanborough Park, Watford. In September 2001 there were 20,979 members in 246 churches or companies throughout the UK and Ireland.

Adventists operate one college of higher education, two secondary schools and nine primary schools in Britain and Ireland. Primary and secondary school enrolment is more than 1,100.

Adventist beliefs

All Adventist beliefs and teachings are centred on Jesus Christ. For Seventh-day Adventists, Jesus was God in human form. He spoke an everyday language and faced the difficulties that we face. He came and lived what in most ways was an ordinary human life – except that His was sinless.

What Adventists believe above everything else is that the death and resurrection of Jesus have vital relevance to every person alive. Through His death and resurrection Jesus saves humans from their sin and sets them on freedom's road. Then He makes available the power to stay free.

Where does the name Seventh-day Adventist come from?

Seventh-day Adventists accept the Bible's account of the origin of this world and of humanity. They believe that God created the universe and all life. They do not subscribe to the view that we evolved or that life merely happened by chance.

Adventists believe that, scientifically, there is ample reason to accept the Biblical account of creation and they feel strongly that the explanation of the flood fits the evidence of fossils and geology as well as or better than the evolutionary hypothesis. The human race has intrinsic dignity and purpose because we were created. We did not just happen.

Seventh-day Adventists also accept God's decision to set aside the seventh day as a perpetual reminder of His creative act. That is why Moses recorded the commandment 'Remember the Sabbath day to keep it holy. For in six days the Lord made the heavens and the earth... Therefore the Lord blessed the Sabbath day and hallowed it'.

That explains the Seventh-day part of their name – they keep the seventh day of the week (Saturday) as the Lord's Sabbath, as distinct from Sunday, which is the first day. They believe it is significant that Christian people be seen to acknowledge God as Creator and Redeemer in this way. They know Jesus did the same, and they believe there is nothing in scripture to suggest that this day was changed for any other. They believe the day is important because it is the only one God has specified that people remember.

Adventists keep the Sabbath from sunset on a Friday to sunset on Saturday. In the winter, particularly in the north, sunset can be quite early. In some cases, this may mean that a child would ask to be excused early from school. This is something that the Church officially supports. The same applies to trips or activities arranged on Saturdays – Adventist children would generally want to be excused.

Seventh-day Adventists accept the Bible's prediction of the destiny of this world. They do not accept the notion that circumstances are going to get better and better, or that humanity can work out its own survival. The Bible makes it clear that conditions are going to grow steadily worse until they totally disintegrate. The only safe resolution is the one described by the Bible. Jesus will return, literally and visibly, so that the whole world will hear and see His arrival. He will resolve mankind's problems. He will restore the world to God's original plan. It will be a place without sin, illness or death. God will dwell with humankind in a 'new heaven and a new earth'.

This explains the Adventist part of their name. Advent refers to Christ's first and second coming. Since they believe what the Bible predicts about the destiny of the world, they call themselves Adventist.

What makes Adventist beliefs different?

Although Seventh-day Adventists claim no formal creed as such, they have developed a Statement of Fundamental Beliefs that sets out their understanding of essential Bible teaching. Most of this statement is the same as that held by all conservative Christians, for example, the doctrines of God, Jesus, the Holy Spirit, the Trinity, the Scriptures, sin and salvation.

Not all Christians agree with one another in every single respect. Baptists, for example, disagree with Methodists, just as the Anglicans disagree on some matters with Presbyterians or Roman Catholics. Areas of discussion within Christian denominations include baptism (Immersion or sprinkling?), the human will (Is it free or are we predestined?), immortality (Do we have it automatically or is it a gift from God?), the Sabbath (Was it for Christians or just the Jews?), and the ten commandments (Were they abolished or are they still relevant?).

In some of these matters, Adventists find themselves in agreement with Methodists; in others, with Baptists or Pentecostals, Anglicans or Catholics, and so on. Most importantly, they believe they stand on what the Bible teaches. This may not always place them with the majority, but nor does it mean they stand alone.

Adventists would prefer that these differences should not drive a wedge between themselves and other Christians. They would rather live in peace as brothers and sisters in God's family, agreeing to disagree without considering themselves to be superior or inferior.

There are some areas of Christian thought which are unique to Seventh-day Adventists, including their understanding of Jesus' work as High Priest in heaven, their concept of the judgement, their understanding of prophecy, and their special mission in this world to present God as the Creator of the universe. However, Adventists would not want these issues to become causes for argument with other Christians.

Lifestyle differences

Because the Bible teaches that the human body is sacred to God, Adventists make deliberate decisions to avoid anything that weakens or endangers it. So they steer clear of alcohol, tobacco, recreational drugs, and caffeinated drinks. These are lifestyle decisions that make a great deal of medical good sense with immediate benefits to all-round health. For the same reasons, they choose not to eat foods which the Bible classifies as unclean (animals described to be carrion scavengers, consuming dead, decaying or effluent matter).

If you have an option, Adventists suggest, it doesn't make much sense to eat such kinds of meat. Many Adventist people go a step further and choose a vegetarian diet because it is more healthy. But none of this is done with the hope of winning reward from God. It is because they believe it makes sense to live as healthily as possible. As they see it, having a healthy body has an impact on the health of mind and spirit.

Adventists also think it makes sense for Christians to control what goes into their minds as well as their bodies, so they try to be careful in what they view or do in leisure time. They avoid forms of entertainment that may erode the Christian's connection with God. They try to be careful about things they do and the places they go to. They look to benefit the character and the disposition, rather than put them at risk. Control and modesty in how a Christian dresses, how a Christian seeks recreation and leisure, and how a Christian generally behaves, creates better all-round health and peace of mind, say Adventists.

This means that some Adventist parents may feel strongly about certain books – *Harry Potter*, for example, though there are no official recommendations. Some may object to books which encourage acceptance of gay relationships – as a Church they promote the nuclear family. However, they do not have any policy on withdrawing children from classes when the issue is raised.

John Surridge, Communication Director, British Union Conference of Seventh-day Adventists.

Useful addresses and books

- For more information on the Seventh-day Adventist Church, visit their website at: www.adventist.org.uk or contact the Communication Director, John Surridge at: British Union Conference of Seventh-day Adventists, Stanborough Park, Watford, WD25 9JZ. Tel: 01923 672251. Website: www.adventist.org.uk
- Publications include: *The Messenger*, an internal fortnightly Church paper.
- The Adventist Development and Relief Agency (ADRA) is an agency established by the Seventh-day Adventist Church for the specific purposes of community development and disaster relief.

Sikhism

With as many as half a million followers in the UK, Sikhs are a growing section of British society.

Sikhism was started by **Guru Nanak** in India in the state of Punjab in 1469 CE. Nine living Gurus followed him, who taught and practised the Sikh teachings in their daily lives. The Gurus wanted to show that although the high ideals they taught are difficult to live by, they are wholly practicable. The tenth Guru, Guru Gobind Singh, declared that after him, Sikhs should follow the Sikh scripture as they would a living Guru.

Today, Sikhs live all over the world. Sikh men are easily recognisable by their turbans and beards and Sikh women by their long hair, left loose or tied neatly in a bun at the back of the head. Sikh men and women wear five symbols, which can be called the uniform of their faith. Each symbol begins with the letter 'K' in the Punjabi language, so they are called the five Ks. They are:

Kesh – uncut hair
Kara – an iron bracelet
Kangha – a wooden comb
Kachera – cotton undershorts
Kirpan – a sword.

These outward symbols make Sikhs stand out in a crowd and link them to the principles of their faith. These being:

The oneness of God
The oneness of humanity
Equality of women
Tolerance towards other religions
Service to humanity.

What Sikhs believe
Sikhs believe in one God, who is neither male nor female but is imageless, formless, does not give birth and never dies, is present everywhere, and is the creator of the universe.

Sikhs are taught that: 'There is but one God who is the truth, and is the creator of this universe. God is without fear and without enmity, is not born and does not die to be born again. God is beyond time and immortal. God is self existent and is by grace revealed'. (Page 1 of Guru Granth Sahib.)

Sikhs believe that God is not exclusive to any one religion. Different religions are different paths leading to the same reality. This does not mean that all religions are the same or equally relevant for all. There are different routes for people to choose

and Sikh Gurus emphasised the right of people to choose their own path through life.

Sikhs are taught to respect other people's views and show tolerance towards those who do not agree with the views of Guru Nanak. The subsequent nine Gurus practised these teachings to show their importance in life. The English meaning of the word tolerance is too weak to fully express this kind of tolerance. In Sikhism it implies a readiness to lay down one's own life for the sake of others, like Guru Tegh Bahadur, the ninth Guru, who was martyred for defending the rights of others. When Hindus were forced to convert to Islam by the Mughal rulers in India, Guru Tegh Bahadur gave his life defending their right to worship in the manner of their choice.

Given that Sikhs believe there is one God who has created the universe, it follows that all human beings belong to one family of God. Guru Nanak in his first sermon said there is neither a Hindu nor a Muslim, only human beings. God is not interested in labels, only how people behave. Guru Gobind Singh, the tenth Guru, writes: 'Recognise there is only one race and that is of all humanity'.

The gurdwara – a place of worship
The Sikh place of worship is called a **gurdwara**. It is open to anyone and everyone who wants to pray to one God. Everyone sits on the floor regardless of social status. There are no assigned places or reserved areas. Men and women are given equal position. Sikh women take equal part in leading services and conducting ceremonies.

Anyone who believes in the Oneness of God and wants to worship can join the Sikh congregation or Sangat. No one can be barred on the basis of caste, religious belief or sex. There are no special holy days or specific times for Sikhs to pray. In England, the congregation usually gets together at the weekend. There is no priesthood so any male or female who can read the Sikh scripture, Guru Granth Sahib, and is knowledgeable about Sikhism can take the service. However, as volunteers do not always have time, the gurdwara management committees appoint staff to conduct services, ceremonies and festivals.

Each gurdwara has a **langar** (common kitchen). After every service the congregation eats together to show that people of diverse backgrounds belong to the one family of God. No distinction is made between rich and poor, giver and receiver. Men and women of all classes and colours prepare and serve food for everyone. This also emphasises the fact that housework is the joint responsibility of men and women.

The Guru Granth Sahib – the Sikh scriptures

Sikhs believe that the highest authority is God. His truth is revealed through the Gurus and is contained in the **Guru Granth Sahib** – the writings of the Gurus and followers of Hindu and Islam whose views were similar to the Gurus. Since scripture takes the place of the living Guru, it is treated with the utmost respect and is central to the Sikh way of life, its ceremonies, festivals and code of conduct.

The Guru Granth Sahib occupies the most revered place in the gurdwara. It is covered with a rumalla (a cloth), resting on cushions on a dais, with a canopy above it. A member of the congregation remains in constant attendance and waves a chauri (a traditional fan or whisk).

The worshippers enter the presence of the Guru Granth Sahib without shoes and with their heads covered. They bow before the Guru Granth Sahib and touch the floor with their heads before sitting down. These are the marks of respect shown to the teachings contained in the Guru Granth Sahib.

Three golden rules or Three Dimensions

Sikhs must remember the three golden rules. They are:

Nam japna – to remember God
Kirat karni – to earn one's living by honest means and hard work
Vand chhakna – to share with others who are less fortunate.

Nam japna is meditation on the qualities of God. It is not a mechanical repetition of the hymns (shabads), but it is necessary to understand their meaning, and act on what they teach. Sikhism teaches that prayer should go alongside working life. To live a good life Sikhs must constantly work to improve society. As the Guru says: 'There can be no worship without performing good deeds'.

Kirat karni is to work hard to earn one's living. A Sikh should lead a family life and its responsibilities. While earning their living they should meditate on God's name. Sikhs should

work by honest means to pay for basics and must not beg or exploit others to become rich.

Vand chhakna is to share one's earnings. The other aspect of this is sewa meaning serving others. Sewa is to help everyone whatever their colour, creed or gender. Sewa can mean giving money, time or using one's expertise.

Diet

There are no restrictions on what Sikhs can eat, except they are forbidden to eat ritually killed meat such as Halal or Kasrut. Food in the langar is always vegetarian.

Dress

There are no rules about what Sikhs must wear, except that men must cover their hair with turbans and boys wear patka, the smaller version of a turban. Because of the patka and turban, Sikhs, particularly young boys, meet a lot of prejudice and can be mistaken for girls. Adults need to be sensitive to this.

Dr Kanwaljit Kaur-Singh, Ofsted inspector

Kirat karni – Guru Nanak's story

When he was travelling, Guru Nanak came to Emnabad and accepted an invitation from a humble carpenter, Lalo, to stay with him. Bhago, a wealthy man, decided to give a feast and invited all the rich and famous people including Guru Nanak. But the Guru did not attend the feast. Bhago asked the Guru, 'Why have you refused to attend my feast'? The Guru replied, 'Lalo's simple bread is earned by honest labour. You have grown rich by exploiting the poor and your food is stained with their blood.' 'Nonsense!' Shouted Bhago in an angry voice.

The Guru smiled. He then took a piece bread from Lalo's house in one hand, and a piece of bread from Bhago's in the other, and squeezed them both. Milk dripped from Lalo's bread and blood from Bhago's! The rich man realised his mistake and promised the Guru to devote his life to helping the poor and needy.

Vand chhakna – Sewa (an example of service)

During a battle between the Mughal Emperor's forces and Sikhs, Kanahya was providing drinking water to the wounded. Some Sikh soldiers complained that he was giving water to the enemy's soldiers and he was charged for helping the enemy and brought before the Guru. But he explained to the Guru, 'I do not see a friend or a foe, but only human beings'. The Guru was pleased with the answer and blessed Kanahya for his true Sikh spirit and his understanding of duty and service.

Common festivals

- Guru Nanak's birthday. The date for this varies by lunar calendar, but it generally falls in November.
- Guru Gobind Singh's birthday generally falls in January.
- Baisakhi – when Guru Gobind Singh gave Sikhs the 5Ks is on 14 April.
- Diwali (when sixth Guru helped release of 52 princes for freedom of worship) – November.
- Martyrdom of Guru Arjan – June.
- Martyrdom of Guru Tegh Bahadur – November.

Chinese New Year: Yuan Tan

Many nurseries and pre-schools care for children of Chinese descent and Chinese New Year is a colourful festival with a story that provides many activity ideas.

Background

Religion in China is complex and derives from a mixture of Buddhism, Confucianism and Taoism with some ancestor worship as well. Some of these elements can be seen in the New Year celebrations.

The date of Chinese New Year is based on the oldest known lunar calendar which has a 12-year cycle, though some additional Chinese festivals follow a solar calendar, particularly where agricultural events are celebrated. It is generally around the end of January to mid-February.

Chinese New Year marks the start of one of three new accounting periods when all debts must be paid. About a week before the festival begins, the family will get together to worship the Kitchen God, Tsao-shen, whose picture is posted above the stove. They believe that he takes an annual report on each family member up to heaven, so honey is smeared on the lips of the portrait to ensure he takes a good report. Sometimes wine is used instead in the hope that he will be so drunk that he will be denied access to heaven! The paper image is then burnt, symbolising the god's ascension to heaven. The house will be thoroughly cleaned and then on New Year's Eve, a new picture will be hung above the stove to welcome Tsao-shen's return. This will be accompanied by fire crackers – originally made by burning hollow bamboo stems, but now commercially available crackers are used.

New Year's Day is a family time. Everyone wears new clothes, and sweets, cards and flowers are exchanged. Children are given red 'lucky bags', **lai see**, which contain small amounts of money.

Food is an important part of the celebrations, though many families avoid eating meat or fish, and no sharp objects are handled in case of accidents which would be an unlucky start to the new year. Mottoes in red and gold – colours associated with good luck – are hung on the doorways with good luck messages and the ancestors are worshipped by burning incense and gifts of food, drink and money to serve them in the afterlife.

A well known part of the celebrations is the lion dance. Groups of dancers, often from a martial arts centre, dance through the streets, the front dancer carrying a lion's head

Chinese zodiac calendar

Year	Year	Animal
1998	2010	Tiger
1999	2011	Hare
2000	2012	Dragon
2001	2013	Snake
2002	2014	Horse
2003	2015	Sheep
2004	2016	Monkey
2005	2017	Cockerel
2006	2018	Dog
2007	2019	Pig
2008	2020	Rat
2009	2021	Ox

The festival story

This story explains how the years were given their names.

Buddha was wondering which animal to choose to name the first year after. The ox was strong and powerful, but the pig was very hospitable and kind. Perhaps it should be the horse or dog? He just could not decide. Then he had a brainwave! He would hold a race to see who would be the first to swim across the river. The winner would be the one after whom the first year was named.

The animals all lined up at the river bank.

The Buddha sounded the signal – and they were off. The dog took an early lead but quickly tired. The sheep was doing well but his fleece became heavy with water and it slowed him down. The tiger didn't like getting wet at all and the dragon was worried because the water kept putting out his flames.

Eventually, the powerful ox took a clear lead. Buddha was sure he would win. Then, just as the ox reached the river bank, the rat sprang onto dry land. He had slyly hitched a lift on the ox's back without anyone seeing him!

The animals felt quite put out but rat was the first on the bank and so the first year was named after him.

The 12 animals of the Chinese calendar are: rat, ox, tiger, hare, dragon, snake, horse, sheep, monkey, cockerel, dog, pig.

and the others being his tail. Accompanied by drums and fire crackers, the lion visits homes and shops, where the owners have hung heads of lettuce containing lucky bags with money. The lion swallows these, spits out the lettuce and 'eats' the money! This dance is believed to get rid of evil and bring good luck in its place. Often a dancer, dressed as Mi-Lo, the Buddha to come, precedes the lion.

The celebrations end with the lantern festival.

Festival activities

- Draw a dragon with a separate tail and play 'pin the tail on the dragon'. (Each person takes a turn to be blindfolded and then tries to pin the tail in the right place on the dragon.)

- Make a lion or dragon using cardboard boxes, crepe paper, ribbons and tinsel with material for the body. Do a lion dance to the beat of a drum.

- Make masks of the animals in the story: rat; ox; tiger; hare; dragon; snake; horse; sheep; monkey; cockerel; dog and pig.

- Organise some races.

- Make lanterns out of a rectangle of coloured paper. Fold the paper in half and make cuts from the folded edge to within 1.5cm of the other edge. Open out and stick the two shorter ends together, then add a strip of paper across the top as a handle.

Sticky cake (steamed Chinese fruitcake – Nian Gao from Northern China)

Much of the food eaten for the festival has symbolic meaning. For example, the names of some foods sound similar to characters with lucky connotations, while the shape or colour of other foods symbolises properties such as happiness, prosperity and good fortune. Kumquat plants, which are popular presents, are considered lucky because of their little golden fruits.

This Chinese fruitcake is a traditional dish served at New Year. It is fed to the kitchen god before the close of the year in the hope that he will take a good report to heaven. The cake is either a bribe or, as I prefer to think, his mouth is so full of cake that he cannot talk at all!

Ingredients
- 2 eggs, with whites and yolks separated
- 35g (1/4 cup) butter
- 50g (1/2 cup) brown sugar
- 100g (1 1/4 cups) glutinous rice flour
- 100ml (1/3 cup) milk
- 125g (1 cup) Chinese dried fruits, pitted if necessary and diced (I used dried prunes, apricots, dates and luxury dried fruit and candied peel.
- 1 piece crystallised ginger, diced (optional)
- 30g (1/2 cup) chopped walnuts.

Method
Grease a loaf tin that is approximately 4 x 8 inches and set aside.

Beat the egg whites until stiff.

Cream together the butter and the sugar. Add the egg yolks and mix thoroughly.

Add one third (a little less than 1/2 cup) of the glutinous rice flour and mix. Add about half of the milk.

Continue adding the rice flour and the milk alternately until the entire amount is mixed in.

Stir in the dried fruits and then fold in the beaten egg whites.

Pour the cake batter into the loaf tin and steam, covered, for about one hour.

Allow to cool and cut into thin slices.

- Make lai see (lucky bags). Talk about New Year resolutions.

Christine Howard

Holi: festival of colours

The Hindu festival of Holi falls on the full moon in the month of Phalgun, which spans the end of February/beginning of March on the Gregorian calendar.

Festivities start on the eve of Holi when bonfires are lit in keeping with the legend of Prahlad. The bonfires are built from all the dried leaves and branches left from winter as a way of cleaning up and making way for spring. The fire represents the destruction of evil – the burning of Holika, a mythological character. The heat is a reminder that winter is over and that hot summer days lie ahead.

The main event of Holi is a carnival of colours when everyone is in high spirits. Crowds of people, many dressed in white, throng the streets and smear each other with brightly coloured powders called gulal and squirt coloured water at one another through pichkaris (big syringe-like pumps). They exchange greetings, the elders distribute sweets and money, and everyone sings and dances to the rhythm of drums.

Messy colours

Note: This activity is best carried out outside. Make sure children are dressed appropriately, either in old clothes or waterproof aprons. Be firm about the rules for squirting water – aim only at the targets and not people.

Talk about the Holi celebrations and how people gather in the streets and squirt each other with brightly coloured powders and water. Provide clean, empty squeezy bottles (the kind used for washing-up liquid, shampoo and lemon juice).

Gather the children around and show them how to fill their containers with water from a bucket, then how to add a few drops of food colouring (use a different colour in each bottle). Discuss the changes to the water. Encourage vocabulary such as change: mix, dilute. Secure a top to each bottle and label it with the correct colour.

Set out several targets (these can be made from paper plates) and ask children how they might aim the water at the targets.

Demonstrate how to squirt the water and encourage the children to experiment. Do the bottles work best when full?

The legend of Prahlad

Holi is associated with the legend of Prahlad, a story that signifies the victory of good over evil. King Hiranyakashipu was an ambitious ruler who wanted absolute power so that he could be worshipped as God. The King's own son, Prahlad, who was a devout follower of Lord Vishnu, refused to obey his father. This made the king so angry that he decided to punish Prahlad. He asked his sister, Holika, for help. It was believed that Holika was immune to fire and could never be burned, so the king asked Holika to sit in the centre of a bonfire with Prahlad on her lap. The bonfire was lit and young Prahlad sat in Holika's lap, praying to Lord Vishnu. His belief saved him, leaving him untouched by the flames but Holika was burned to ashes. To mark this legend, huge bonfires are lit on the eve of Holi.

When they hold them in a certain way? Set up new targets and repeat the exercise, trying out different bottles and colours.

Holi hand flowers

Show children how to trace an outline of their hand onto a coloured piece of paper. Encourage each child to do this and cut out their hand shape. Using a pencil demonstrate how to roll the fingers up so that they curl. Curl the hand shape vertically into a trumpet/lily shaped cylinder with the finger curls curling outwards. Staple the flower onto a drinking straw, along with a few cut-out leaves. Discuss how the flowers signify those that are collected and dyed during Holi.

On a large piece of backing paper draw a faint tree outline for children to paint. Glue each child's hand flower to the tree (you may wish to accompany the flower with the child's name label). Finally add a title in large letters: 'Our Holi tree'.

Colours from nature

Explain to children that, traditionally, the colours used at Holi came from nature – from flowers. Tell them that they are going to make their own colours from flowers and water, just like Hindus do at Holi time.

You need:
- Tesu flowers: half a kilo
- a strainer/sieve.

Dried tesu flowers are available in some markets. You can look for them in grocery stores or shops that sell Holi colours. But you could also try this activity with flowers from the children's own gardens or make natural dyes from beetroot or blackberries (though be careful as these will stain).

What to do:
Pass some of the flowers around. Encourage children to smell their fragrance, feel their texture and describe the colours and shapes. Provide magnifying glasses for closer inspection. Point out the intricate details of the stem and petals.

Let children watch as you carefully fill a bucket half-way with boiling water. Pour the flowers in and explain that you are going to leave them to soak overnight. What do they think might happen?

Next day, help children to strain the mixture into a bowl. Demonstrate how to make squeezing movements using your fist. You should now have a yellow-ish orange mixture. Explain that this is just like the paint used to spray people at Holi. It is ideal as it does not have any harmful effects on the skin.

Holi banner
Make a 'Happy Holi' banner from strong coloured paper to hang from the ceiling. The children can decorate it with brightly coloured stickers and confetti.

Give each child a sheet of plain paper, crayons, pens, markers and other colouring materials. Ask them to draw and colour a picture of what the holiday means to them. They might want to draw some Holi flowers, chapatti bread, or perhaps people decorated with bright shades of paint. Add the finished drawings to your banner as a vibrant welcome sign for visitors to your setting.

Allison Hedley

Useful websites
- http://www.holihangama.com/ (Offers brief history of the festival.)
- http://www.theholidayspot.com/holi/ (Includes links to historical and cultural information, traditional recipes and modern celebrations.)

Dosti chapati (Indian friendship bread)

- 2 cups flour
- pinch salt
- 1 tbsp oil
- warm water to mix.

Method
Mix ingredients, adding enough water to form a stiff dough. Pinch off two small pieces of dough, each about the size of a walnut. Roll out to a small circle, about 8cm (three inches) in diameter. On one side of one circle, smear a little oil, put the other circle down on the oily side, and press down lightly. Dust with dry flour. Roll out the two circles, now stuck together, to make a big circle.

Put the chapati on the hot pan. When one side seems cooked, turn it over to the other side and bake. Discuss with children how the size, colour and texture change as the chapati starts to cook.

Press down gently with a clean cloth, if needed, to ensure even cooking. Take the chapati off the heat, and separate the two. They should pull apart easily because of the oil you smeared on them before cooking.

Fold each chapati into a triangle and keep covered in a clean cloth until you are ready to eat them.

Makes about 20 to 22 chapatis – perfect for snack time!

Shrove Tuesday: 'The Runaway Pancake'

This well-known story has been enjoyed by generations of children. These activities would make the perfect follow-up to a Shrove Tuesday celebration.

Start by telling children that most cultures and religions have their special days, and on Shrove Tuesday, pancakes were a way of using up all the eggs and fats before **Lent**, a period in which many Christians still give up eating certain food.

Telling the story

Read or tell the story 'The Big Pancake' or adapt a similar story, such as 'The Gingerbread Man'. 'The Big Pancake' tells how a mother and her seven hungry boys make a large pancake, which slips from the pan when it is being tossed and rolls away. It is chased by the mother and children who shout 'Stop! We want to eat you!' One by one, the family are joined by a man, a cat, a cockerel, a duck, a cow, and finally a pig, who tricks the pancake into rolling onto its snout to be carried across the river, and instead gobbles it up.

Help children understand the basic structure: how it starts, what happens next and how it ends. Trying to remember which characters chase the pancake, and in which order, encourages their ability to sequence events.

Using the story

After making your own pancakes together, help children to make up their own story by asking them what might have happened if one of their pancakes had run away. Who would it meet? The caretaker? A passing dog? The crossing patrol lady/man? Scribe their ideas onto a flip chart and then, together, retell the story, starting with 'Once upon a time, a teacher (or use your own name) and her hungry children made a very big pancake...'. Encourage children to join in shouting 'Stop! We want to eat you!' at the appropriate time, and ask them to suggest what the pancake said in reply.

Once children are familiar with their new story, help them to role play the different characters. Scribe the words 'Stop! We want to eat you!' on to large cards and encourage children to 'read' them with you.

Creating story books

Involve each child in drawing a different picture of one part, or one character, of their new story. Scribe or help them write a short sentence underneath, so that together the pictures tell the story. Glue the pictures and sentences in order in a large sugar paper book.

Discuss how to make a suitable cover for the book. Ask them for a title, the authors (the name of their group), and how to illustrate it. Encourage them to read the book independently in the book corner.

Brenda Williams

Recipe for pancakes (makes 12)

- 125g plain flour
- pinch of salt
- 2 eggs, beaten
- 260ml milk
- 1 tbsp sunflower oil, for frying
- lemon and sugar to serve.

Method
Sieve the flour and salt into a mixing bowl and make a well in the centre. Break the eggs into a small bowl, beat, then pour into the flour.

Pour in a third of the milk and start mixing.

Add the rest of the milk, a little at a time, beating well after each addition.

The mixture should be smooth and the consistency of single cream.

Wipe the frying pan with kitchen paper dipped in oil to coat the surface, then fry the batter.

Note: Children can be involved with measuring and mixing but will have to watch you cooking the pancakes as the pan must be very hot to make sure they are crisp.

The Runaway Pancake

Being able to talk about an event, or retell a story in the right order, is an important skill for children. It helps them to organise their thinking when they later start to write independently.

This traditional story, which is similar to 'The Gingerbread Man', tells of a big pancake which escapes from a family of seven little boys and their mother. As it runs away, it is chased by a man, a cat, a cockerel, a duck, a cow, and finally a pig, who tricks the pancake into rolling onto its snout to be carried across the river, and instead gobbles it up!

Encourage children to enjoy retelling the story in their own words, using the pictures below to help them.

The Christian festival of Easter: The Last Supper

Many young children will be familiar with Easter – but few will know that it is an important Christian festival with a deep religious meaning.

In the Victorian era, families were large and infant and child mortality was high. Death was an everyday occurrence and bodies were laid out in the front parlour for friends and families to visit and pay their last respects. By contrast, today people seem to be afraid of even talking to the recently bereaved, presumably in case it might upset them.

As a general rule, Western society finds the subject of death difficult to handle.

Talking about death

Young children do not often come face to face with death on a personal level, though they are bombarded with images of death through the media.

Some religions have highly developed rituals surrounding mourning and death. In Judaism for example, the family of the bereaved 'sit shiva'. This is when the close relatives of the deceased spend the seven days following the burial at home, where they sit on low stools and receive visitors. Shiva comes from the Hebrew word 'Shevah' meaning seven. This is a time when friends can offer their condolences and talk about the loss. Most of the bereaved want to talk about the deceased and this ritual encourages it.

Children need to be able to express their feelings and fears about loss and death. There are a number of good books which help them to do this through story. Many of them stress the importance of remembering. (See also page 40.)

One way of helping children to grieve is for them to make a 'Remembering book' where they can include pictures and photographs of the dead person along with their own feelings, thoughts and memories.

Many people feel that the crucifixion is too hard for young children to cope with. Yet the Easter story does not make sense without it. The story of the Last Supper links the themes of death and remembering with Easter and life.

Easter biscuits (makes approx. 20 biscuits)

- 224g flour (plain or self-raising)
- pinch of salt
- 1/2 tsp mixed spice
- 84g butter
- 84g caster sugar
- beaten egg
- 84g currants.

Method
Turn oven on at gas mark 3 or 170°C. Sieve flour, salt and spice together. Cream together butter and sugar until light and fluffy. Beat in egg. Add flour to bind to a firm paste. Stir in currants. Make into small balls, flatten slightly and place on a greased tray allowing space between them to spread. Brush with milk or water and sprinkle with caster sugar. Cook for 20 minutes.

Background to Easter

Easter is a spring festival the date of which is based on a complicated solar calendar. It may fall any time between late March to late April.

It is the most important of the Christian festivals as it embodies many of the fundamental Christian beliefs such as God's intervention in human history to save mankind from sin and death by the death and resurrection of His Son, Jesus. Through this act Christians believe He confers on them eternal life. Thus the Friday on which Jesus died is called 'Good' (Great in Orthodox churches).

The festival of Easter comes at the end of the fast period of 40 days known as Lent. This begins on **Ash Wednesday** and the day before is **Shrove Tuesday**, popularly known

The festival story

It had been a busy week. John Mark had been there when his hero, Jesus, rode into Jerusalem on a donkey. He had waved his palm branch wildly and shouted at the top of his voice 'Hosanna!' with the rest of the crowd. Now it was Thursday and Jesus was coming to John's house with his friends for a special meal.

Later that evening, after he had helped his mother prepare the room at the top of the house, he crept upstairs to listen at the door. Jesus was there with his 12 friends. They were seated around the table and Jesus was talking.

John Mark peered around the door. He saw Jesus take some bread and heard him say: 'Baruch atah Adonai, Elohenu melech ha-olam' – 'Blessed are You O Lord Our God, King of the universe…' but what was he saying now? 'This is my body which is broken for you. Do this in remembrance of me.' Later, Jesus held up a cup of wine and said a prayer, adding 'This is my body which is shed for you. All of you, drink'. John Mark was puzzled. What did it mean? He knew this was bread and wine. How could it also be body and blood?

As he was trying to work it all out, the door burst open, knocking him against the wall. He was just in time to see the back of Judas rushing down the stairs. Inside, the meal was over and the rest of the family had joined Jesus and his friends to sing hymns of praise. John Mark came out of hiding and joined in too. He was so happy sitting there in the glow of the oil lamps with all his favourite people.

The religious leaders were afraid of Jesus and wanted to kill him. They paid Judas to tell them where Jesus would be. So, later that night, Judas led some Roman soldiers to arrest Jesus. They put Jesus on trial, because they said he called himself a king and there was only one king, the emperor in Rome. Although what they said wasn't true, Jesus was found guilty and sentenced to death by hanging on a cross. How sad Jesus' friends felt on that Friday.

Yet on the Sunday, those same friends were happy. They came to believe that Jesus had returned from the dead and was alive. Many of them claimed to have seen him and even had a meal with him. They believed that he was God's own Son. John Mark also believed. When he was older, he told the story of Jesus to his children and they told it to their children and so on, until today. Those people who still believe are called Christians. In their churches they share bread and wine and remember what happened at Jesus' Last Supper. They celebrate Jesus coming alive at their festival of Easter.

as Pancake Day (or Mardi Gras on the continent). Pancakes were made to use up all the eggs, milk and butter before the start of the Lenten fast. Christians went to church to be shriven or have their sins forgiven. Next day, Ash Wednesday, palms that were handed out the previous year on Palm Sunday are burnt and the ash placed on the forehead of the penitent. It was traditional not to eat meat, eggs or other luxury foods during Lent, and to eat fish on Friday. Today most people only choose to give up a luxury like sweets or alcohol.

Palm Sunday is the Sunday before Easter. It marks the start of Holy Week. This reflects the time that Jesus rode into Jerusalem on a donkey while the crowds shouted 'Hosanna!' and waved palm branches in celebration. Churches often hold processions and hand out palm crosses.

On **Maundy Thursday**, the Last Supper is recalled. This is the basis for the service of Mass, Eucharist or Communion which most Christian churches celebrate today. Maundy Thursday is also associated with the washing of the disciples' feet described in John's Gospel. In some churches, it is followed by the Gethsemane vigil, when worshippers remember the time that Jesus prayed in the garden of Gethsemane, before he was arrested.

Good Friday recalls the day of the crucifixion with the death and burial of Jesus. Then Easter Sunday is a day of celebration of the Resurrection of Jesus from the dead.

The story is found in all four gospels in the New Testament part of the Christian Bible.

Festival activities

- Read and talk about *Badger's Parting Gifts*.

- Make a 'remembering table' with objects, photos and pictures of people we remember.

- Make an Easter garden.

- Listen to a recording of the 'Hallelujah Chorus' from Handel's Messiah.

- Decorate an egg – use a real egg or paint a paper egg.

- Bring some pots of flowering bulbs into the warm and watch them grow throughout Lent. Talk about new life.

- Arrange an Easter egg hunt.

- Make and eat hot cross buns or Easter biscuits.

Christine Howard

Helping a child cope with loss

Everyone has to face loss at some stage in their life and you may need to help a young child cope with losing a relative, friend or pet. Story books can help.

Pets

It is important to be honest with children about the life-span of pets, especially hamsters and gerbils, as they often only live for two or three years.

Losing a pet is often a child's first experience of death but it can be intense. They need lots of opportunities to talk about how they feel and share memories. It may help to have a simple service to say goodbye. Don't dismiss children's grief. Help them to express it.

Some children can seem quite callous about the death of a pet and after a very short time be asking for a new kitten. Again, this is normal and should not be condemned.

Relatives

When a grandparent or close relative dies, young children are often confused and bewildered by their own feelings and the grief of those around them. They might ask repeated questions and need lots of reassurance. It is important to be as honest as you can when answering them.

Many young children confuse death with sleep and you need to help them realise that there is a difference even if it is painful.

It often helps children to be involved in some way in saying goodbye at a funeral service or other ritual. Some families compile a special book of photos and memories for their child to keep.

Friends

Children occasionally have to face the death of a friend or sibling due to illness or accident. Again, it is so important to allow children opportunities to talk about their memories, draw pictures, and be involved in saying goodbye.

- In the picture book, *Badger's Parting Gifts*, Badger's friends think they will be sad forever. But gradually they are helped to remember him with joy and to treasure the gifts he left behind for each of his special friends.

Judith Harries and Ruth Andrews

Useful books

- *Badger's Parting Gifts* by Susan Varley (Andersen) ISBN 978-1-84939-514-4
- *When the World was New* by Alicia Garcia de Lynam (Lion) ISBN 978-0-74594-271-1
- *Grandma and Grandpa's Garden* by Neil Griffiths (Red Robin Books) ISBN 978-1-90543-409-1
- *Always and Forever* (Corgi) ISBN 978-0-55256-765-7
- *Help me say goodbye* (Fairview) ISBN 978-1-57749-085-2

Art and craft for Easter

Art and craft is at the heart of good early years practice as it engages children in a physical, emotional, social and intellectual activity.

Cheeky chicks and daffy ducks

Easter wouldn't be the same without them! Think tiny with this activity to focus on fine motor skills. You will need either yellow cotton wool balls or two sizes of yellow ready-made pompons.

Make a chick or duckling with two pompons joined by glue, a folded paper beak, beady painted eyes and card feet, which can be prepared by an adult.

With close supervision, the youngest children can take a little PVA glue on a spreader and touch the surfaces to be joined gently so that there is not an overload of glue.

For the eyes, use black acrylic paint and tiny pointed brushes, taking a tip of paint to dot onto the pompon head.

Display sets of chicks and ducklings in their own nests made from covered shoe boxes or small baskets filled with shredded brown tissue paper, soft hay or wood shavings. (Be aware of allergies to hay and shavings.)

Help children count the chicks in each nest and write numbers on large broken-egg shaped labels. Discuss what the baby chicks might look like if they grew up. You could tell a short version of *The Ugly Duckling*, involving children as winter winds, unkind farmyard hens and the returning swans.

I'm the Easter Bunny!

For a personalised Easter card, fold an A4 piece of white card in half, then take digital photographs of each child's smiling, cheeky face and cut out the head only. If you take two

Read Shirley Hughes' *Out and About* (Walker Books) for beautiful poems and pictures of springtime.

This Little Puffin compiled by Elizabeth Matteson (Puffin) has traditional Easter poems, songs and rhymes to do together.

or three children, head and shoulders, side by side, in landscape format, they will be a manageable size for the card if printed on A4 size paper. The face needs to be about 10cm deep.

Help children stick them onto the front of the card and draw big bunny ears on top of their photo head. They can add an oval bunny body, tail and legs. Draw green grass and a huge spring sun. Write 'I'm the Easter Bunny! Happy Easter!' inside for them to add their own marks to or to copy under.

Pop-up chick or bob-up bunny

To make a chick pop up from its egg you need a polystyrene cup, a lolly stick and a pompon chick (as above). Make the chicks but leave off the feet.

Turn into a rabbit by adding tiny card ears and three painted dots for eyes and nose.

Leave the pompon figures to dry then glue a long lolly stick to the back of the body and base of the head. An adult can cut zig-zags in the top of the cup for the chick's egg but leave the bunny's hiding place plain and make a neat slit in the base of the cups for the lolly stick to go through. Cut the cup down if necessary, depending on the length of the stick.

Rhona Whiteford

The Jewish festival of Passover

Although many schools and nurseries explore the Jewish festival of Hanukkah with children, the festival of Passover or Pesach is more important to Jews.

Signs and symbols are an integral part of religious language. People use metaphor, analogy and symbolism to talk about God. These sound like theological concepts that are far too complex to tackle in the Foundation Stage, but even the youngest children are used to dealing with signs and symbols.

Before they can read, they recognise a variety of everyday symbols from the McDonald's logo to the branding on their favourite toys. Understanding that a collection of shapes (letters) stands for their name is an important step in learning to read. Passover is a festival full of symbolic significance and a good place to start.

Background

Passover or **Pesach** could be described as a founding festival as it marks a watershed in the development of the Jewish faith, the point at which God ratifies the promise or covenant that He made with his chosen people (the Jews) through Abraham, and lays on them the obligations of that covenant in the form of the ten commandments.

The date of Passover is based on a lunar cycle and so is not fixed. It takes place around March or April. It celebrates the freeing of the Jewish people from slavery in Egypt and was probably originally a spring festival.

The festival lasts for eight days (seven in Israel). During this time no yeast (chametz) may be eaten, so in the time leading up to the festival Jews are busy spring cleaning to remove all traces of yeast from the house. Households use special Passover crockery and cutlery and *matzot*, similar to water biscuits, replace bread.

The highlight of the festival is the **Seder** when the family gets together over a festive meal and relives the events of the Exodus, the coming out of Egypt, which took place more than 3,000 years ago.

At the centre of the table is the Seder plate. In Hebrew the word seder means 'order' and the meal follows a set order. The plate has divisions for different symbolic foods. These are:

- A burnt egg representing new life and the freewill offering at the Temple. It is burnt as a reminder that nothing is perfect.

- Horseradish as a reminder of the bitterness of slavery.

- Lettuce which is sweet but then bitter, to represent how sweet life was when the Jews first entered Egypt but then turned bitter with slavery.

- Charoset, a mixture of apple or pomegranates, nuts, wine and cinnamon, representing the mortar from which the Jews made bricks.

- Parsley or a green vegetable, another reminder of spring and new life. It is dipped in salt water representing the tears of the slaves.

- A lamb shank bone, a reminder of the blood of the lamb which was smeared over the doorposts of the homes of Jews so that the Angel of Death would 'pass over' their houses and spare their first-born sons from death.

Recipe for macaroons (makes approx. 18 biscuits)

Matzo meal is used in place of flour during Passover. If it is not available, crush matzot biscuits finely or use ground rice or semolina instead.

This recipe is not suitable for people with nut allergies.

- 1 egg white
- 112g ground almonds
- 112g caster sugar
- 1 tsp fine matzo meal (or ground rice or semolina).

Method
Turn oven on at Gas mark 6 or 200°C.

Beat egg white until stiff. Mix sugar, almonds and meal together. Add egg white and form a dough. Make into small balls about the size of a walnut, flatten slightly and place on a greased tray, allowing space between them to spread. Cook for 10-15 minutes until lightly coloured. Decorate with half a blanched almond (optional).

The order of the night is written down in a special book called the Haggadah or 'telling'. This tells the story of the first Passover, including the ten plagues which God sent on the Egyptians to persuade them to let His people go. At the mention of each plague a finger is dipped in a glass of wine and spilt on a serviette as a reminder that God is always sorry when any part of His creation suffers.

During the meal four glasses of wine are drunk representing the four freedoms or promises God made to the Jews: 'I will free you from slavery; I will redeem you; I will take you as my chosen people; I will give you a land of your own'.

There is plenty for children to take part in. They hunt for chametz before the festival to make sure that the house is clean from all leaven or yeast. They find the afikomen, a piece of matzot which the father has hidden during the meal. They open the door to look for Elijah, the great prophet who will come before the Messiah, God's Anointed One. The youngest child asks certain questions which allows the host to explain the festival and the evening ends with the singing of festival songs.

Festival activities
- Make a Seder plate out of a paper plate and make traditional Passover foods using matzo meal.
- Spring clean the classroom.
- Go on a treasure hunt for something hidden, like the search for the chametz or matzah.
- Learn some Passover songs such as 'Dayenu' ('It is enough').

Christine Howard

Useful books
- Sam's Passover (A & C Black) ISBN 978-0-71364-084-7
- Let My People Go by Lynne Broadbent and John Logan (RMEP) ISBN 978-1-85175-210-2. Also available as a big book (RMEP) ISBN 978-0-82257-241-1
- Exodus storybag available from Articles of Faith Ltd.

Artefacts and resources
- Seder plate, children's Haggadah.

DVDs/videos
- Animated Haggadah (also available as a book); Moses from the Testament series of videos; Moses, Prince of Egypt. Available from Articles of Faith, Suite 105, Imperial House, Hornby Street, Bury, BL9 5BN. Tel: 01992 454 636. Website: www.articlesoffaith.co.uk

The festival story

(From Exodus 1:15, the second book of the Torah).

The Jews had gone to Egypt in the time of Joseph, because there was a famine in Israel. They had been looked after there but when a new pharaoh came to the throne, who did not like the Jewish people, he made them slaves and ordered all baby boys to be put to death.

One mother, JochEbed, tried to save her son by placing him in a waterproof crib and floating him down the River Nile. He was found by Pharaoh's daughter who decided to keep him and brought him up as a prince in her father's palace.

One day, this young man, who was called Moses, saw a taskmaster beating a Hebrew slave. He was angry and beat the taskmaster to death then hid the body in the sand. A few days later he saw two Hebrews fighting and went to stop them. 'Are you going to kill us like you killed the taskmaster?' they asked. He realised that his secret was out and he ran away from Egypt.

Some time later he was looking after sheep on the hillside when he saw a bush which appeared to be burning but did not burn! God spoke to him from the bush and told him to return to Egypt to rescue his people. He came up with all sorts of excuses but God wouldn't take no for an answer! So taking his brother, Aaron, Moses went to Pharaoh, but he refused to listen. He didn't want to give up the chance of free labour. So God sent a number of plagues, to make Pharaoh change his mind. First, he turned the Nile to blood, then he sent frogs, followed by gnats, flies, animal diseases, boils, hail, locusts, and three days of darkness.

Sometimes, Pharaoh would agree to let the Jews go, but then he would change his mind again. In the end, there was only one thing to do. Moses told Pharaoh the final plague would be the death of all the first-born sons of the Egyptians.

Moses warned his people to get everything ready for a final meal and leave at any moment. The blood of a lamb was to be smeared over their doorposts so that when the Angel of Death came He would pass over their homes. That evening the Angel of Death came and killed the firstborn children of the Egyptians, even Pharaoh's son, but He spared all the Israelite children. Pharaoh was so upset that he agreed to Moses' demands and let him lead his people out of Egypt. At the Red Sea, the water parted so that they could walk across, but when the Egyptians tried to follow, the waters returned and drowned them all. The Israelites from Egypt had started their journey to the Promised Land.

The Sikh festival of Baisakhi

Make this Sikh festival meaningful to young children by giving it relevance to their own lives.

In the past, religious education concentrated on children learning *about* the religion. Facts are easy to teach and relatively uncontroversial. However, if this is all that happens, there is a real likelihood that religion will be seen as irrelevant, and nothing to do with everyday life.

Look for those areas which relate to common human experience, so children can learn from those aspects of the story or religion which touch on their own lives. This makes it relevant and of far greater interest.

An example of this approach, taken from the story of Baisakhi, might be to look at standing up for what we believe to be right. In the classroom or nursery setting it might be a case of seeing a child being bullied. How does the individual deal with this? How should the rest of the class react when they see this happening?

This is the core of the Baisakhi story. Five men were willing to stand up for what they believed to be right. The Sikhs, as a group, were prepared to resist the 'bullying' of the Mogul invaders and to defend everyone's right to hold their own religious beliefs even if they were not the same as the Sikhs.

Background (the Gurus)

Sikhism is the youngest of the religions which are commonly studied in the UK. Although included as a world faith in terms of RE in schools, Sikhism is largely restricted to those whose families originate in the Punjab area of north India. However, many Sikhs became economic migrants to the UK during the 1950s and 1960s and have a large presence in some areas.

Sikhism's first Guru or teacher was Guru Nanak. Born of a merchant Hindu family in 1469, he grew up in a society where Islam was strong, following an invasion of the Punjab by the Mogul emperors in the 16th century. Guru Nanak was also familiar with Jainism, but as a young man he was dissatisfied with what these religions had to offer.

Because Sikhism uses a non-Western script which has no direct equivalent to some letters, many of its words have alternative spellings. Hence Baisakhi can also be spelt Vaisakhi.

Recipe for karah parshad (also karah prasad)

- 100g sugar
- 425ml water
- 100g unsalted butter
- 50g plain flour
- 100g semolina or ground rice.

Equipment:
- Saucepans
- Wooden spoon
- Bowl for serving.

Method
Mix the water and sugar together in the saucepan and bring to the boil, stirring until the sugar has dissolved. Set on one side. Melt the butter in a saucepan over a low heat. Add the flour, beating well with a wooden spoon. Add the semolina or ground rice and continue to beat well. Heat the mixture until the butter separates. Remove from heat and gradually add the sugared water until a stiff paste is formed. (If the mixture becomes too stiff, add a little more butter.) Transfer to a serving dish. Karah parshad or holy food is served at the end of the gurdwara service where it is given to all as a symbol of the Sikh teaching about the sharing of food. It is eaten with the fingers.

Note: All cooking with young children should be closely supervised. Because the sugar syrup in this recipe becomes very hot, it may be advisable for the adult to prepare this part of the recipe and allow the syrup to cool a little before adding it to the other ingredients.

The festival story

In 1699 there was a Hindu festival. Both Hindus and Sikhs were there. So was Guru Gobind Rai, leader of the Sikhs. He stood up on the platform in front of a great crowd and in a loud voice called out for one volunteer who was willing to give his life for his beliefs. Everyone was silent. Again, the Guru called out until finally one man stepped forward. Guru Gobind Rai took his volunteer out of sight. Everyone wondered what was going to happen. Suddenly the Guru appeared again alone but with his sword dripping with blood. There was a gasp from the crowd. What had happened to the volunteer?

Guru Gobind Rai stepped to the front of the platform again and, with his sword held high, shouted out for another volunteer who was prepared to sacrifice his life for his beliefs.

People turned and looked at each other. Was the man mad? Then another man stepped forward from the crowd. He, too, was taken behind the screen and then the Guru appeared alone, his sword red with blood.

In all, this happened five times until the Guru appeared again with the five men alive. 'These men,' he called out, 'were prepared to give their lives for their faith. They are the Beloved Ones or Panj Pyare and they will become the first members of the Khalsa.' Everyone cheered. Then the Guru held up his hand for silence.

'From now on all Sikhs will be called by the same family name to show that we are all equal and no-one is more important than anyone else. The men will be called Singh which means lion, because they will be brave and stand up for the right to believe. The women will be called Kaur, which means Princess.

We will also all wear five special objects so that people will know who we are. These will be the steel bangle or kara to remind us that there is only One God who is eternal; we will not cut our hair, kesh, and we will wear a comb or kangha in it to keep it tidy. We will wear special shorts known as kacchera so it will be easier to ride on a horse in battle and we will carry a knife or kirpan to defend ourselves and others in danger, but it will never be used to attack anyone first.'

That is exactly what happened. Guru Gobind Rai became known as Guru Gobind Singh and even today many Sikhs are still called Singh or Kaur. Those who are members of the Khalsa also wear the five Ks, the special objects given to them by Guru Gobind Singh. (They are called the five Ks because each one begins with the letter K.) That is also the reason why Sikhs wear turbans – it keeps their long uncut hair tidy and in place.

One day, however, it is said that he was bathing in the river before meditating, when he was carried off to the heavenly court where he was told to preach the divine Name: Nam. This was the start of a new community of disciples or Sikhs, who followed his teaching, sang hymns and practised meditation.

Guru Nanak was succeeded by nine other Gurus. The tenth Guru, Guru Gobind Rai, who later became Guru Gobind Singh, was of great importance as he established the Khalsa, or community of Pure Ones, in an event which is celebrated every April at the festival of Baisakhi.

The festival story is gory and will need to be adapted for very young children. No-one actually knows what happened. Some people believe a miracle took place and that Guru Gobind Singh decapitated his volunteers and then brought them back to life. Others take it in a far more symbolic way and say that the people believed the volunteers were being killed but it was, in fact, animal blood on the Guru's sword and the five men were unharmed. The point is that the men were prepared to sacrifice their lives, even if they didn't have to in the end.

Guru Gobind Singh was the last of the Gurus. He said that after he died the only Guru the Sikhs should have would be their holy book, which was put together in 1604 by the fifth Guru, Guru Arjan. This original copy is called the Adi Granth or first Granth and it is kept in the Golden Temple at Amritsar, in the Punjab.

If you ever visit a Sikh gurdwara or place of worship, you will see the **Guru Granth Sahib** (holy book) on a special platform and it is treated as if it were a very important person. You will probably also be able to see a picture of the Golden Temple of Amritsar.

Festival activities

- Talk about what it means to be brave. Discuss standing up to bullying and developing these strategies with the children.

- Look at a map of the world and find the Punjab in north west India/Pakistan. Punjab means five rivers, so find the five rivers of the Punjab and look for the holy city of Amritsar, where the Adi Granth is kept.

- Make a special book/talk about special books.

- Make some Asian sweets to celebrate Baisakhi, or try making karah parshad, a special sweet mixture made with semolina and sugar that is distributed at the end of each Sikh service.

- Build a Sikh home corner and furnish it with Sikh artefacts, for example pictures of the Gurus and the Golden Temple; sarees; kameeze and shalwar; a Sikh doll with the 5 Ks; Asian cooking utensils. Sikh homes do not have a copy of the Guru Granth Sahib unless they can dedicate a special room to it.

Christine Howard

Celebrating May Day

Learn about an ancient festival and have fun!

In the weeks leading up to May Day, talk to children about the signs of new life as spring begins. Examine buds as they open, look for signs of birds building their nests and lambs in the fields. Ask children's families to tell you about May Day when they were young. They may have some photographs you can display.

Celebrate May Day in your group by asking children to wear their best clothes. Make crowns from card and cover them with flowers made from tissue circles scrunched up in the centre. If you have a good supply of flowers get the girls to bring in hair bands and wind ribbons around them to make head garlands. Flowers can then be stuck to these with sticky tape around the stalks.

Morris men wear straw hats covered in flowers so the boys can cover old hats in straw and attach flowers. Alternatively they could make a simple headband and cover this with flowers. The children can wear garlands around their necks. Take a long piece of string and tie a cardboard disk to the end. Cut out crepe paper circles and pierce a hole in the centre of each one. Thread the circles onto the string.

Villages often hold a 'Hoop Competition' for the best decorated hoop. The children could decorate some hoops by winding strips of crepe paper around them and using sticky tape to attach real or paper flowers. Hang the hoops up as mobiles to decorate your May Day room.

Maypole and Morris dancing are traditional May Day entertainments. Teach your children some simple ring dances such as 'Round and round the village' (This Little Puffin) or simply dance around in a big circle to some music. Many of these country dances involve a bow or curtsy at the start or finish of the dance. Talk to children about the tradition of 'Honouring your partners' in this way.

Morris men wear bells on their ankles. Sew some small bells to ribbons and tie them to the children's ankles. Experiment with the sounds the children can make. Try tip-toeing and stamping. Cut out some large squares of white material for children to wave as they dance. Knocking sticks together can be dangerous but let some children have pairs of wooden claves to create a traditional sound as they dance.

Maypole dancing is exciting and satisfying and the ribbon patterns grow as the dance progresses. Talk to children about how these patterns are made and make some plaits with ribbons or plait doll's hair to demonstrate this.

What is May Day and why do some people celebrate it?

May Day is an ancient festival dating back to Roman times celebrated on 1 May, marking the coming of spring after the cold winter months. It is associated with flowers and dancing to symbolise the start of new life.

In medieval times May Day was a public holiday with much fun and family enjoyment. Traditional customs arose from this celebration such as the crowning of the May Queen and maypole dancing.

In the nineteenth century the first of May became known as Labour Day, a public holiday with processions and celebrations throughout the world. Many country villages traditionally celebrate May Day today. At the start of the festivities a May Queen is chosen and she reigns for the day, attended by several of the village children. She wears a floral crown and sits on a throne covered with flowers. It is a chance for all the girls of the village to wear their best dresses.

Maypole dancing takes place on village greens. Coloured ribbons are tied to the top of a maypole and village children hold a ribbon and dance around it, weaving in and out of each other and creating patterns as the ribbons wind round the pole.

Morris dancing is also popular on May Day. The name originates from the Spanish 'Moresco' dancers of the thirteenth century. These men blackened their faces so that evil spirits would not recognise them. Today they do not always do this but they still bang sticks together, stamp their feet and wave handkerchiefs vigorously in the air to represent the triumph of good over evil as the summer replaces the winter.

Jean Evans

Maypoles and Morris men

Celebrate May by making a maypole and doing your own version of Morris dancing. It's not as complicated as it sounds – just follow these simple steps and movement ideas.

Morris dancing has been a traditional type of folk dancing in Britain for centuries. It is likely that the name derives from 'Moorish'. Some believe that it was introduced from Northern Africa or medieval Moorish Spain, around the 14th century. It is more likely that the dance is much older than its name and had been danced in Britain since ancient times, and that the term 'Moorish' was used because the dancers often blackened their faces (to disguise themselves). They therefore looked like 'Moors', the only black race familiar to medieval Europeans.

Morris dancing originated as a pre-Christian fertility or luck-bringing dance and was for men only, but these days women also join in the many groups that can be seen at local festivals and events throughout the summer.

The dancing would start in May time and continue throughout the summer to celebrate British festivals such as May Day, Oak Apple Day (29 May) and Mid-summer.

Alongside Morris dancing are all the traditions around May time celebrations, especially maypole dancing and 'bringing in the May'. I have concentrated on combining elements of each of these to suggest ideas for you to enjoy with young children. The aspects of Morris dancing that would be fun to bring to a pre-school are the costumes and bells, fluttering handkerchiefs, decorated ribbon sticks and rattles and, of course, the skipping and hopping movements that characterise this form of dance.

Key movements to concentrate on with the children to give them a physical vocabulary in these dance forms are: skipping, hopping, stamping and waving.

Skipping

Skipping can be tricky for young children. At the age of three, some can skip and others can't. Don't try to teach them – it will come naturally in time. Let children see you skipping and find their own response to the skipping rhythm.

Skipping rhythms are lilting and often jerky (for those of you familiar with musical terms, 6/8 is a typical skipping rhythm). The simple rhythm of 'Jack and Jill went up the hill' fits perfectly into this category. Other well-known

nursery rhyme tunes that can be used for skipping include 'Hey diddle diddle', 'Skip to my Lou' and 'Pop goes the weasel'. (For any Radio 4 fans, the theme tune to The Archers is perfect skipping music!)

The beauty of using song to skip to is that you can all sing or hum along as you skip and adjust the pace to whatever suits.

Instruments

To accompany your skipping music, have a group of children as the band playing the shaker bells, and possibly add in a drum or tambour yourself. (One that you can carry as you move with the children.) If the children seem to respond confidently to the rhythm, add in one or two children playing drums as part of the band. A circle is the best way to start, and holding hands helps to maintain the shape. Try skipping around in one direction for a whole verse of your song, then stop and skip the other way while singing a whole verse once again. The children will learn to measure the length of time they skip around each way and will be able to anticipate a change of direction. When they become accomplished at this, you could try changing direction half-way through each verse.

In Morris dancing you often see two lines of dancers facing each other. This game explores the relationship of the partners to each other, as they approach each other and then back away.

- Ask children to find a partner.

- Give them grouping names ie partner A is an orange, B is a lemon. (This makes it easier for you to address either of the lines at any time.)

- Clearly define two straight lines on the floor by chalking, using a marking that exists in the carpet pattern already, a line of masking tape or even drawing an imaginary line for them to observe!

- Ask all the oranges to stand on one line and the lemons on the other, making sure that they stand opposite their partners. (They may need a little help the first few times.)

- Define a line half-way between the two groups (chalk, ribbon, rope).

- When you're ready, ask both lines of children to walk to the middle line, say 'hello' and shake hands with their partners, then go back to their places. As it is only a few steps either way, they should be able to manage walking backwards to their starting lines (demonstrate the action first). Repeat this a few times, then start to make a game of it by giving different instructions. Walk to the middle, meet your partner and:

  O wave to each other
  O jump up and down
  O stamp your feet
  O clap your hands
  O clap against your partner's hands
  O twizzle around together holding hands.

You can extend this game to become hop, skip and jump!

When children have become used to the set of actions and the pattern of meeting in the middle, you can vary the style of movements as they come to the middle to meet their partners.

- Hop to the middle and shake hands.

- Jump to the middle and shake hands.

- Skip to the middle and shake hands.

If you are varying the hops, skips and jumps, it is probably best to stick to the same action in the middle each time so as not to confuse them. They return to their places by walking the few steps backwards to reach their lines.

All of these versions of the game can be played without music, the children responding to the spoken command. However, once they have built up their skills and become used to the spatial pattern of moving towards each other and back again, you can either find some recorded music or sing a song and have the children dancing towards each other and back again in time to the music.

It's up to you whether you add any claps or actions in the middle. With older or very capable children, you can extend the dance by leading each line around and through an arch as you would if you were playing 'Oranges and lemons'.

Introducing props

The real fun starts when you start introducing props! Try to find some recorded folky type music that's fun to skip to and let children skip around freely in the space enjoying the props.

Hankies

Give children handkerchiefs (or pieces of sheet cut up), one in each hand. Play 'Morris says', a game based on 'Simon says' to help build up their movement vocabulary. In this version nobody need be out – just carry on with the fun if someone moves on a command that starts without 'Morris says'.

Morris says: Wave your hankies high in the air above your heads.
Morris says: Wave them down by your sides.
Morris says: Wave one high and one low.
Wave them to the side.
Wave them near the ground.
Wave them to the sky.

Bells

Rather than put bells on elastic garters which could be uncomfortable or slip on little legs, try fastening individual bells to shoes; these will jangle delightfully when they dance around. Use any sets of jingle bells you have to play along with the rhyme:

Ride a cock horse to Banbury Cross
To see a fine lady upon a white horse
With rings on her fingers (shake hand bells)
And bells on her toes (Shake bells on shoes)
She shall have music wherever she goes.

This would be a perfect opportunity to add a hobby horse, another feature that often appears in traditional Morris dancing.

Hoops and garlands

Traditionally, children would get up early on May Day and gather branches from trees that showed the first blossom, often the hawthorn (May blossom) tree. They would wind these into knots or garlands and carry them through the streets for good luck and in the hope of collecting money. Hence the song, 'Here we come gathering nuts in May' which was originally 'knots' (nuts are not ripe in May). Why not decorate a hula hoop or a hoop made from a stick cut from a hazel tree? These are bendy when cut young and can easily be wound around into a circle.

Ribbon sticks

These can be with or without the balloon shakers on the top.

Materials: a stick of some sort, about a third of a metre long (this could be a kitchen roll tube, a piece of dowelling, a length of hazel cut from a hedge or a section of plastic water pipe).

Ribbons

If you don't want to use real ribbon, cut strips from crepe paper, coloured plastic carrier bags or oddments of fabric.

Prepare the ribbons in advance by sticking a piece of sticky tape to the top of each one and sticking them in a long line to the edge of a table, radiator (switched off) or a window. This avoids sticky tape frustrations when working in a group. The children can then pick a ribbon one at a time (with the tape already attached) and can concentrate on trying to stick them on to the end of their sticks.

If you have a shaker, add this last! Traditionally this would have been a blown-up pigs bladder!

Shakers

Put some dried beans in a balloon and blow it up but not to its full extent. Tie a knot in and tape it to the top of the ribbon stick. Although the children will not be able to blow up the balloon and tie it themselves, they can be involved by putting their beans into the neck of the balloon while you hold it and they can choose the colour of their own balloon.

Note: Besides the focus on circles and straight lines meeting partners, let the children have plenty of opportunity to dance around freely with the props in response to the music and song.

Making your own maypole

If you can do maypole dancing outdoors all the better. Rather than attempting to dance around it holding ribbons and weaving in and out together, revert to the original tradition of dancing around the decorated pole without the entanglement of holding ribbons.

What you need

Ideally use a branch or pole and fix it into the ground safely. (The main trunk of a discarded Christmas tree with all the branches cut off is suitable if you can remember to save it next year!) Your pole could be tall and straight but a beautiful branch with lots of little side branches might be more satisfying for small children to decorate. Other alternatives are to use a garden parasol base with a length of broom

handle wedged into it and a large cardboard tube slotted over the top. The children can paint and later stick decorations onto the tube.

Decorate with:
Ribbons: traditionally the colours were yellow to represent the sun, blue to represent the sky and green to represent new growth (you will often find red ribbons, too).

Flowers: real or otherwise.

Other: brightly coloured wool wound around branches, bundles of herbs, coloured flags and handkerchiefs.

The men usually wear white and decorate themselves with bells and ribbons. Waistcoats could be worn – red, black or green. Trousers would be knee-length, so children could tuck trousers into long socks to look authentic. The women would wear flowing skirts in red, black or green; white blouses and sometimes shawls. Both men and women might wear straw hats decorated with flowers.

Maypole dancing

Small bands of musicians would play – often a combination of a hand-held drum or tambour, a piano accordion or squeeze box, a fiddle (violin), and simple wooden flutes or recorders.

If you can find a volunteer to come and play on any one of these instruments for you all to dance to, it would make a wonderful addition to your May dancing. However, singing for yourselves and/or recorded music will work well, too.

Once you have been working on the different aspects suggested by Morris and maypole dancing, you could create a special celebration.

If conditions permit, it would be lovely to dance on grass barefoot. The children will be able to feel the earth and you can talk about the coming of summer and how things will grow in the earth now that it is beginning to warm up. You can tell them that people in the past celebrated May Day because of this, because it was the beginning of the time of year when crops and flowers would grow to make food for them.

Dress up, dance around your decorated maypole, dance to the music waving hankies and ribbon sticks, wear ribbons in your hair or garlands on your head, shake bells, wear bells, skip, hop, jump, clap your hands, stamp your feet, dance in circles, first one way then the other, dance into the middle, dance with your partner, swinging around.

Have a person with a hobby horse to ride amongst you and tease and chase you. Sing 'Here we come gathering nuts in May'. Have special treats to eat – a picnic or some fruit arranged in baskets with ribbons tied around the handles.

● Find an old umbrella and take away the material covering.

For children to do

● Ask children to draw pictures of themselves. So that they are big enough, use comparative measuring, that is ask them to make their picture as big as ... their own foot or a grown-up's hand. (Use your hand for them to measure against.)

For you to do

● Stick the figures onto pieces of different coloured thin card and cut them out.

● Attach each figure on a small length of ribbon or cotton to the end of each umbrella spoke. (If the spoke ends are unprotected by plastic tips, bind them with strong tape to pad them out or put corks on before you attach the figures.)

● If you like, you can decorate the umbrella by weaving ribbons around the top and the handle and attaching flowers (real, artificial or paper) or any other decorative bits and pieces you may have handy.

The children will love to see you twirl the umbrella and see themselves dancing around in a circle.

Chrys Blanchard

The Buddhist festival of Wesak

The Buddhist philosophy of meditation and denial of the self is difficult for young children to grasp but there are elements of the faith that everyone can relate to and these are the areas on which it is best to concentrate.

Religious belief is a dynamic, vibrant way of life for many believers. The best way for anyone to understand what faith means is to talk to someone within the faith. DVDs and videos, though one step removed, are a useful source but few are available for young children. Artefacts are a third important means of gaining insight into faith.

Using artefacts

Artefacts need to be approached with care and sensitivity. It is important to know which items are cultural or fun or practical, and which are treated with reverence or respect by the believer, so that you can convey this to children.

Hopefully, most children are taught from an early age to respect other people's property and that some things are to be treated with respect because they are special. These feelings of awe can be fostered in the way that you introduce artefacts.

One way is to ask children to bring in a picture or talk about something which is special to them or someone in their family. You may wish to share something which is important or special to you. The artefact can then be introduced as something which is special to some people. You might keep it covered and then unveil it to introduce an element of suspense and anticipation, or reverence and respect.

Some artefacts are suitable for handling, with others you may wish to adopt a 'look but do not touch' policy. Explain the reasons for this. It may be to show respect, but it could be for practical reasons, too, in the case of a fragile but expensive artefact.

Introducing a Buddha rupa

A *rupa* (statue) of the Buddha is an example of an artefact that should be treated with respect. A Buddha *rupa* is not a toy to be played with, so why not put it on a special shelf or table and decorate the area with pictures of flowers? You may like to create an area similar to a Buddhist shrine. If so, you need to make it clear to the children that this is what it

would look like in the home of a Buddhist or in the *vihara* (Buddhist place of worship) but it is not part of what they do, unless of course, they are Buddhists themselves.

If you have a child of that faith in your class, your job is much easier, because you can make the distinction concrete: 'This is what X might have in her home'. Another way would be to use a book showing a child of the faith with the artefact in its setting.

Eight treasure rice (Babao Fan)

This is a popular sweet rice recipe which can be eaten on any Buddhist festival.

The rice contains eight treasures or charms to keep evil away. They could also represent the eight-fold path of Buddhist teaching.

- Boiled rice (made from 2 cups of uncooked rice)
- 2 tablespoons butter or margarine
- 3 tablespoons brown sugar
- 8 different varieties of fruit and nuts (dates, almonds, raisins, dried apricots) for the treasures.

Method
Grease a pudding basin and put alternate layers of rice with fruit and nuts. Make sure that the fruits can be seen at the edge once the pudding is turned out of the bowl.

Cover with foil and steam for 40 mins.

Turn out on to a plate and decorate with nuts.

Check for any food allergies before sharing this with the children.

The festival story: Prince Siddhartha achieves Enlightenment

Prince Siddhartha was a rich young man who had everything. When he was born, his father, the king, had consulted a fortune teller, who predicted that the prince would either be a great ruler or a holy man.

The king did not want his son to be a poor preacher so he tried to stop the prince leaving the palace and its gardens by giving him everything he could possibly want.

It was true that Siddhartha lived in a magnificent palace, wore the most expensive clothes and was married to a beautiful wife who gave him a fine son. He had servants who waited on him hand and foot, and there was nothing that he wanted that he could not have. Yet he wasn't happy. Being rich was not enough. He wanted to know what was beyond the palace walls.

One day, Siddhartha left the palace in his chariot. He was amazed at the world outside. On his travels he saw an old man. He did not know that people grow old. On another day he saw a sick man. He had never seen anyone who was ill before. He went out again and this time he saw a dead man. Up to this time Siddhartha had not known that all beings eventually die. He began to wonder about why we are sick, grow old and then die.

He went out one last time. This time he met a holy man who spent his life praying and fasting.

Siddhartha returned to the palace but he was still not happy. He thought about the things that he had seen. What did it all mean? Finally he had had enough.

'I must find an answer to this', he said to himself. So one day, he left his wife and son and set out to try to find the meaning of the sadness and suffering he had seen.

He became a holy man. He wandered into the forest, dressed in poor clothes and hardly ate. He became dreadfully thin but he still didn't know the meaning of the signs.

Finally, he decided that this wasn't working, so he tried another way. He started eating again, put on proper clothes and sat down under a tree to think.

After a long time, the answer came to him. He realised why there was suffering in the world. From this time on he was called the Buddha by his followers. It means the Enlightened One.

Background

Buddhism is an ancient religion which came from Nepal, north-east of India, and takes its name from the title of its first teacher, the Buddha. Buddha means the Enlightened One and is a term used of anyone who attains a state of enlightenment. However, in popular thought it is associated with Siddhartha Gautama, a young Indian prince, born around 563 BCE*, who formulated and preached the precepts of Buddhism.

Wesak is one of the major Buddhist festivals. It celebrates the birth, enlightenment and death of Siddhartha, which are said to have taken place on the same day of the year, at the full moon, usually in May. (Wesak is the Sinhalese name for the month.) Lamps play an important part in the celebrations because of their association with enlightenment, so lamps are hung and in some parts the bodhi tree is circled with lamps. The local temple is also decorated and Wesak cards are sent. Buddhists from different parts of the world may celebrate this festival in different ways according to their local culture and traditions.

Festival activities

- Talk about things that make people sad. Discuss why this is and what we can do to help.

- Make Wesak cards. Birds and flowers make good decorations.

- Make Wesak lamps out of clay or Plasticine or use foil cake holders. Use night lights in the lamps and stand them in sand for safety. Alternatively make a lotus-flower holder from card to hold at night.

- Make a Wesak lantern out of paper and decorate with birds or flowers, or make a frame of green garden sticks and cover with tissue paper. **Safety note: Do not put lights inside paper lanterns!**

- Paint lotus flowers – the lotus is a symbol of enlightenment, or draw a mandala. A mandala is used as an aid for concentration to help the mind to reach enlightenment. It is usually in the form of a circle and brightly coloured. Tibetan and Nepalese Buddhists believe that colours symbolise different parts of the mind. Mandala patterns are usually symmetrical. (Example at website:www.graphics.cornell.edu/online/mandala)

- Talk about the rules which we all need. This could include classroom rules. The children could make up their own list of positive rules, for example be kind to each other (rather than do not hurt each other).

- Try sitting quietly cross-legged on the floor. Listen to the sounds around or concentrate on a single object, such as a lighted candle.

Christine Howard

* BCE stands for Before Common Era. Like many non-Christians, Buddhists use this term instead of BC (Before Christ).

The Hindu festival of Raksha Bandhan

Most early years settings have a home corner where children can develop creative and expressive play. These are also the ideal place for children to experience elements of a different home culture.

With appropriate guidance, children can become familiar with objects from a variety of cultures and so learn to respect and value differences in the practices and, ultimately, the beliefs of others. At the same time, they will discover shared values and practices.

Hindu home

If you are focusing on a particular festival, such as Raksha Bandhan, you could turn your home corner into a Hindu home. Include cooking utensils such as those for rolling out chapattis. Put a carpet on the floor and encourage children to remove their shoes, explaining that this is common practice in Hindu homes. Encourage children to suggest why this might be.

Put up pictures of popular Hindu deities such as Krishna, Lakshmi and Ganesh. If possible, have some photos of a Hindu family in traditional dress and provide appropriate dressing-up clothes.

Play Indian music, particularly that with traditional instruments like the sitar or tabla, and include Indian Hindu

Recipe: Easy cook kheer

- 1 tin of rice pudding
- 4–5 cardamom pods
- Small handful of raisins
- 1 tbsp cashew nuts finely chopped.

Method
Soak the raisins in hot water for a few minutes, then drain.

Open tin and place rice pudding in a microwaveable bowl. Stir in cardamom and raisins. Heat for 2 minutes, stir and heat for another minute (cooking times may need to be adjusted).

Leave to stand for 1 minute and sprinkle with cashew nuts to decorate.

Remove cardamom pods before eating. May also be eaten cold.

Traditional Hindu society

Traditional Hindu society is divided into four main castes: the Brahmins or priests; the Kshatriyas or warriors and nobles; the Vaisyas or merchants and the labourers or Shudras.

Within these castes there are also subcastes and these dictate what job a person can do and who he or she can marry.

There were also those who were outside the caste system, called outcastes or untouchables. Gandhi worked hard to have this category removed.

There is a rite of passage for the males of the first three castes which involves the wearing of a sacred thread or janoi, actually three strands of cotton. It takes place between the ages of eight to 12 and signifies a second spiritual rebirth.

dolls. Make sure you include a number of picture books relating to stories from the Hindu tradition.

You might also think about reserving an area in the home corner for a Hindu home shrine, as no practising Hindu home would be without one. You could introduce it by telling a story associated with the Hindu *murti* (statue) in the shrine, most commonly Ganesh. This will give you the chance to talk about respect and how to treat the shrine.

You will need to make it clear that this god is special to Hindu children not everyone. This is much easier if there are children in the group who are themselves Hindu, so you can have a conversation along the lines of 'You might find a shrine like this in Sita's home because she is a Hindu, but not in (for example) Muhammad's home because he is a Muslim and his family do not worship Ganesh'.

You can use a similar approach with other religions. However, bear in mind that there are some items associated with some religions which either wouldn't be found in the home (for example, a Christian chalice and paten) or which are too sensitive to be left out unattended, such as a Muslim Qur'an.

The festival story

Lord Krishna, who was the god Vishnu in human form, had two sisters whom he loved dearly. Subhadra was his sister by birth but Draupadi was his adopted sister.

Subhadra was jealous of Draupadi and one day she came to Krishna complaining that he did not love her (his real sister) as much as he loved his adopted sister. 'My dear sister', he said, 'Love isn't like that. You cannot demand love. Those who show the most love are more likely to receive love. Now I know that Draupadi loves me.' Subhadra was angry. She shouted as she left him, 'That's just not fair! You know I love you better. I would do anything for you.'

Some time later, Krishna had an accident. He cut his hand so badly that it wouldn't stop bleeding. He went to Subhadra for help, who said: 'Hmm. It is a bad cut, but there is nothing I can do about it. Maybe I ought to go and find a bandage for it.' and she left the room. Time passed but Subhadra did not return.

As Krishna was wondering what he should do, Draupadi, his adopted sister, came in. She took one look at Krishna's hand and immediately tore a strip off her own saree and used it to bandage the hand and stop the bleeding.

So which sister loved Krishna more? Subhadra, who was his real sister or his adopted sister Draupadi who helped him when he needed it? (By the way, Subhadra never did return with a bandage!)

There are a number of duties to be observed with the handling of the Qur'an, so an alternative might be to have a Qur'an stand with a book of Muslim stories about the Prophets on it instead.

Background to the festival

The origin of Raksha Bandhan is unclear. One suggestion is that it comes from the story of Indra, a war god. His wife tied a rakhi round his wrist so that whenever he wore it in battle he would be unharmed. He went into battle and defeated the evil demons, thus winning back his celestial abode.

Others believe that the idea stems from the great Hindu epic, 'The Mahabharata'. In this the warrior Abhimanyu was given a protective amulet by his grandmother. As long as he was wearing it he came to no harm, but it broke in battle and he was overpowered by his enemies.

The modern festival originated in the seventeenth century at a time when the Mogul invaders carried out atrocities on Hindu women and they needed protection.

Nowadays it is a happy festival. Because extended families are common in Hindu society (for example, when a young girl marries she goes to live with her husband's family), cousins are regarded as brothers or sisters and included in the custom.

The day starts with an early bath, after which *Puja* (worshipping of god) takes place. The sister offers aarti to her brother and ties the thread on his right wrist. Then sisters and wives give a *rakhi*, a simple bracelet or amulet, traditionally made of silk, to their brothers or husband. The *rakhi* is tied on to their right wrist to protect them and also to enlist their protection. (Raksha means protection and Bandhan, to tie.)

In return, the men give them a gift, perhaps a new saree or some sweets, depending on their age and circumstances. They place a tilak mark on each others' foreheads and share some Indian sweets such as barfi (see recipe on page 59).

This is also the time when the family priest or Brahmin may visit and receive gifts and the Brahmin (the priestly caste) and other 'twice born' Hindus change their sacred threads.

Festival activities

● Make rakhis to give to someone special.

● Make and eat sweets like barfi (see recipe on page 59).

● Talk about families and how they look out for each other.

● Discuss how we can help people we love.

● Hold a *rakhi* party and exchange *rakhis* and sweets.

Christine Howard

Celebrating harvest: Harvest Festival and Sukkot

Thanksgiving for harvest is a common theme in world faiths but you need to be aware of the roots of the various festivals and what they have come to represent.

Festivals from different religions sometimes have what appear to be similar underlying themes. However, it is important to know how these festivals differ, not only in their practice (which may be obvious) but also in the concepts which lie behind the practice.

An easy way to illustrate this is by looking at the various 'festivals of light': Diwali, Hanukkah and Christmas. While it is true that they all take place in the winter and involve lights, the theology behind them is radically different. Diwali celebrates victory over the demon Ravanna; Hanukkah the re-dedication of the temple in Jerusalem and Christmas the birth of Jesus, God incarnate.

Similarly, although thanksgiving for harvest may be a common theme, you need to be aware of the roots of the various festivals and what they have come to represent.

Background to the festivals

Harvest Festival
The celebration of harvest in Britain pre-dates Christian times. People lived close to the earth and were dependent on a successful harvest if they were to survive the winter. Many of the early traditions continued once Christianity came to Britain, with a great celebration taking place when the last of the crops were brought home to the barns. This was known as 'Harvest home'.

Today's practice of bringing produce to church to say thank-you for the harvest is relatively modern, dating back to 1843, when the Reverend Robert Hawker invited parishioners to a special thanksgiving service at his church at Morwenstow in Cornwall.

Sukkot
The celebration of a successful harvest is common to most religions, particularly where they have developed from an agrarian community. It is likely that the Jewish festival of Sukkot (meaning 'booths') was originally a thanksgiving at the end of the fruit harvest, as is suggested by its other name, Festival of Ingathering. However, at an early stage, it became associated with the 40 years when the children of Israel wandered in the wilderness after the Exodus from Egypt.

The festival of Sukkot is marked by the building of booths or huts as commanded in the book of Leviticus (23:42): 'You will dwell in booths for seven days; all natives of Israel shall dwell in booths'. These booths must have at least 2.5 sides and are made of material that has grown but is not still growing. The roof covering has to be open enough to let in the rain and it is good if the occupants of the *sukkah* (pronounced sue kah – this is the singular of *sukkot*) can see the stars. All meals should be eaten in the *sukkah* and in warmer countries Jews

---

Recipe: Tzimmes

This recipe uses fruits and vegetables. Tzimmes are a traditional Jewish dish.

Serves 6 as an accompaniment. Raisins or dried apricots and prunes can also be added at the same time as the apples.

Ingredients
- 3 sliced carrots
- 4 sweet potatoes, sliced
- 3 cooking apples, peeled and quartered
- 100g brown sugar or honey to taste
- 100g butter or margarine
- Salt and pepper to taste
- 250ml water.

Method
Cook the carrots and sweet potatoes until tender. Do not overcook or they will go mushy. Drain and cool. Preheat oven to 180°C, gas mark 4. Grease a 2.5 litre casserole dish. Make a layer of carrots; add a layer of sweet potatoes and then a layer of apples. Sprinkle with sugar, salt and pepper and a few knobs of butter or margarine. Continue making layers until all the ingredients have been used up. Add 250ml of water. Cover and bake for 30 minutes or until the apples are tender. Remove cover and cook until lightly browned.

The festival story

Ruth was hungry and worried. Her husband had died and she had come with Naomi, her mother-in-law to a strange land where she knew no-one. Had she made a mistake? Should she have stayed in her own land with her sister? What would she do for food?

Ruth was clever. She went to Naomi and said 'Mother Naomi, we are hungry. Let me go into the fields and pick some corn to make us some bread.'

'What a good idea', Naomi said, 'but be careful and only go to the edges of the field'. In those days poor people were allowed to gather any corn left at the sides of the field.

Ruth ran off to the fields and began to collect barley. She didn't know that she was being watched by the farmer who owned the field. He thought she was very beautiful, and he felt sorry for her. He called to his workmen and said, 'You see that girl over there? I want you to look after her and make sure no-one tries to hurt her. Let some of the barley fall on the ground so she can pick it up'. The workmen did as he told them.

At the end of the day, Ruth went home to Naomi with her hands full of grain.

'Look, Naomi. Look how much corn I got today. We can make lots of bread with this', she laughed happily. Naomi was pleased but surprised. 'Whose field were you in?' she asked.

'The field belongs to a man called Boaz', Ruth replied. Now Boaz was a relative of Naomi's dead husband. Next day, Ruth returned to pick more barley from the field. Boaz was there and he asked his friends who she was. 'She is the girl who married your dead cousin's son', they told him.

Boaz nodded and carried on watching Ruth. He fell in love with her and arranged to marry her. Everyone was happy. They were even happier when Ruth and Boaz had a baby boy. They called him Obed.

When Obed grew up he had a son called Jesse, and when Jesse grew up he had many sons. The youngest was a shepherd boy. He used to sing songs which he played on the harp. He was also a fine shot with the catapult. He even killed a giant of a man with a stone from his catapult. When he grew up he became a great king. His name was David.

may also sleep in it. It is a time for hospitality so guests are invited to share a meal in the *sukkah*.

In the synagogue special blessings are said using the *lulav* and *etrog*. These are symbolic leaves and fruit, called the 'four species'. The *lulav* is made up of a palm branch, three myrtle and two willow branches bound together. They probably symbolise the final harvest of the year but another interpretation suggests that the palm is for the spine, the myrtle for the eye and the willow for the mouth. The *etrog*, a kind of large lemon, represents the heart.

During the ceremony the leaves are shaken in the direction of the four points of the compass while prayers are said. Again the origin of this practice is not clear but it may be that in Israel the rain begins in autumn and the falling leaves of the willow indicate desire for rainfall to ensure a good harvest the following season.

It has been suggested that it was the Jewish festival of Sukkot which inspired the early Pilgrim settlers in America to create Thanksgiving, a festival of thankfulness for the bounty of their new home.

The story of Ruth, retold here, belongs to both the Christian and Jewish traditions, as it is found in the Book of Ruth in the part of the Jewish Bible known as the Writings. It is a story also commonly associated with another Jewish festival, Shavuot or Weeks, which is a spring harvest festival when the giving of the law is celebrated.

Festival activities
- Make a nature table or harvest display. Remember that harvest can include harvest of the sea.

- Talk about things that we want to say thank you for.

- Sing or listen to a popular harvest song, for example 'We plough the fields' or 'All things bright and beautiful'.

- You may wish to introduce issues of world poverty by comparing what we have to eat with people living in other parts of the world.

- Make a picture using autumn fruits and seeds.

- Try making corn dollies using art straws.

- Create a collage of food to show its origins, for example milk from a cow.

- Make a sukkah from an old cereal or shoe box.

- Make a harvest loaf or dough decorations using a bread mix.

Christine Howard

A poem for harvest time

Most children enjoy listening to the rhythm and rhyme of a poem. The poem 'Farmer, farmer' (see page 58) offers a starting point for a variety of language activities.

On a simple level, children can enjoy and respond to it as a seasonal rhyme. You can use it to extend their vocabulary by exploring the meanings and sounds of new words, and help them develop an awareness of rhyming words. You could extend their understanding of the poem by creating a farm shop in the home corner. Develop communication skills by involving children in discussions and negotiations about their plans, and encouraging them to attempt writing for different purposes, as they make notices or shopping lists. Role playing parts in the shop will stimulate their imagination, and help them to take turns in conversations.

Enjoying and responding to the poem

Begin by showing children some pictures of farms and farmers. Explain that many farmers grow food as well as keeping animals. Help them to understand that in the autumn, many of the crops are ready to eat, and that the farmer has to work hard to harvest them all and store them or send to the shops, before winter.

Read the poem through, and then read it again, discussing and explaining any unfamiliar words such as 'crops', 'dawn', 'baling', 'fading'. Then, in a large space, invite children to pretend to be farmers as they act out the poem. Read each verse, and encourage them to think of ways they can mime it.

Once the poem and actions are familiar, some children will start to join in with the words. Encourage them to emphasise the repetition of the first line, and keep to the beat of the poem. It can be fun to split older groups of children into two, with one group saying a verse while the others mime it, and then changing over for the next verse. This also helps them to remember it.

Using the poem to develop understanding of rhyme

Take a different verse each day and say it together. Then ask children to listen carefully to identify which words have a similar sound. For example, on the first day, with verse one, they should suggest 'crops' and 'shops'. Brainstorm ideas with the group, inviting them to think of other words which rhyme with these words, such as 'hops', 'pops', 'flops', 'tops'.

You can extend this activity with older children by writing each verse out on a flip chart, highlighting the rhyming words by using a different coloured felt pen, and inviting children to read the verse with you, as you emphasise the rhyme. Scribe their suggestions for similar rhyming words on a new page of the flip chart, and ask them if they can create a simple rhyme of their own using these new words. For example, 'Hop hop, Right to the top, Fall to the bottom, Flop flop flop!'

In the other verses, similar rhyming words might include: 'born', 'lawn', 'yawn', 'torn'; 'pay', 'stay', 'tray', 'lay'; 'shell', 'fell', 'bell', 'tell'; 'right', 'fight', 'sight', 'might'; and 'said', 'led', 'fed', 'red'.

Extending the poem into role play

Bring in a selection of typical local farm-shop produce such as the carrots, apples, pears and plums mentioned in the poem, and other vegetables such as potatoes, cabbage, onions and so on. Let children handle the items and talk about their shape, colour, and the things they like or dislike. If possible take children to visit a farm shop.

Involve children in a discussion of how they could set up the home corner as a farm shop. Ask for ideas on making imitation produce – for example, colouring cardboard cut-outs, moulding Plasticine, using clay. Can they suggest ways of displaying their goods? For example, on trays or in cardboard boxes. What clothes from the dressing-up box would be suitable? What kind of notices would they need? Encourage them to think of such things as 'entrance', 'exit', 'car park' and a name for their shop. Depending on their ability, involve them in making their own notices by scribing the words for them to colour in, or letting them write their own. In the same way, show them how to make labels for the different produce, and encourage older children to read them.

Use their ideas in practical activities to create their shop. Provide A4 sheets of paper for children to make lists of items they wish to buy, either by drawing the items, or using emergent writing. Suggest that the shop is used by just three or four children at a time, one as shopkeeper and the others as customers.

Brenda Williams

Farmer, farmer

Young children often show they have a natural sense of rhythm by dancing to music and singing along to nursery rhymes. Many soon develop a delight in words that rhyme.

You can build on this love of rhythm and rhyme by introducing children to other poems with predictable rhyming words and repetitive phrases that they can join in with. This will encourage their listening skills, and develop their confidence in experimenting with new words.

The images created in some poems inspire children's imaginations, and others, like 'Farmer, farmer', give them information about people or places.

You could talk about the images suggested in the poem by comparing the words to the illustrations. The poem gradually leads children through the long day of the farmer at harvest time.

Older children might enjoy cutting out the pictures and muddling them up to make a game of re-assembling them in the right order.

Brenda Williams

Farmer, farmer
Harvest the crops
Put into store
Or fill the shops.

Farmer, farmer
Up at dawn
Out in the fields
Cutting the corn.

Farmer, farmer
Works all day
Digging up carrots
And baling hay.

Farmer, farmer
Fruit to sell
Apples and pears
And plums as well.

Farmer, farmer
Out at night
Driving a tractor
In fading light.

Farmer, farmer
Go to bed!
Time to rest
Your weary head.

© Brenda Williams

The Hindu festival of Diwali

Religious stories are an ideal way of introducing moral issues to young children. The story of Rama and Sita is one of the best known in the Ramayana, the Hindu scripture.

Story is an important element in teaching and learning with young children. It provides opportunity for active learning through role play and drama, art work and creative writing.

Many of the Early Learning Goals can be delivered through story and the non-statutory Framework for Religious Education make this connection explicit in its section on the Foundation Stage. For example, under Personal, Social and Emotional Development ('Understand what is right, what is wrong and why') it says: 'Using story as a stimulus, children reflect upon the words and actions of characters in the story…'

Story provides a non-threatening link through the child's imagination to the real world. Religious stories are an ideal way of introducing major religious and moral issues in a way that enables the listener to relate them to their own experience.

Background to Diwali

Diwali (a word meaning 'row of lighted lamps') is a five-day festival that is celebrated in October/November. It marks the end of one year and the start of a new. The Hindu calendar is based on a lunar cycle, so the exact time changes each year. This is when businesses close their books and pay off any debts in preparation for a new beginning.

On the third day, Hindus offer *puja* (worship) to Lakshmi, consort of Vishnu and goddess of wealth and bounty, in the hope that she will bring prosperity in the coming year. Deva lamps are lit to welcome Lakshmi, and rangoli patterns are made on the threshold of the home in coloured rice powder, sand or chalk to welcome the goddess. Diwali cards may be sent and presents exchanged. New clothes are worn.

Diwali is also a Sikh festival. It commemorates the time when the sixth Guru Hargobind was imprisoned. On his release he asked that 52 Hindu princes who were in prison with him should also be released. The king agreed to let go as many as could hold onto the Guru's cloak. He used a special cloak with many long tassels. All the princes could hold it and so they were all freed.

There are several stories associated with Diwali. They all have a theme of good triumphing over evil. One of the best known is found in the Hindu scripture: the Ramayana, a great Sanskrit epic. It is the story of Rama and Sita. It actually belongs to the festival of Dusshera that precedes Diwali but

Diwali sweets: coconut barfi (makes 24)

- 2 cups (125g) desiccated coconut (or fresh grated coconut)
- 3 tsp ghee (clarified butter)
- 2 cups (300ml) milk
- 1 cup (70g) milk powder dissolved in a little of the milk
- 1/2 tsp ground green cardamoms
- 2 (280g) cups sugar
- 1/2 tsp yellow colouring
- 1/2 cup (30g) chopped nuts (almonds or pistachios – optional).

Method

Lightly fry the coconut till light brown in ghee. Remove from heat. In another pan bring the milk to the boil then add it to coconut with the dissolved milk powder, cardamoms and food colouring. Mix well. Thicken over a medium-low heat stirring occasionally. Add the sugar and nuts if used. Continue to let the milk thicken. It is ready when the mixture comes away from the side of the pan and can be rolled into a ball. Roll it into a large ball and place on a greased plate or tray. Flatten it to a square 1.5cm thick. Alternatively roll it into a number of smaller balls. Leave to set and cut into 3cm squares.

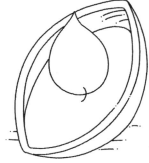

The festival story: Rama and Sita

The brave Prince Rama had married the beautiful Sita. They were very happy together. One day, however, the queen, Rama's stepmother, wanted her son, Bharata, to be king instead of Rama. The queen had once saved Rama's life and he had promised that she could have whatever she wanted in return, so he had to grant her wish. Rama was sent into exile and Sita and another brother, Lakshmana, went with him. Meanwhile unhappy Bharata put a pair of Rama's shoes on the throne to show that it was Rama who was the rightful king.

Rama and Sita went to live in the forest. Rama and Lakshmana hunted for food and they ate wild berries and drank from the forest streams. Life was good, until one day the evil demon King Ravanna, who had ten heads, saw Sita and wanted her for himself. He set about trying to find a way to trick Rama so he could kidnap her!

One day, Lakshmana saw a fine young deer he wanted to catch. So he left the cottage where they lived and went off into the forest. After a while, when he had not returned, Rama heard his brother's voice calling for help. He wanted to help Lakshmana but was afraid to leave Sita alone. Before he left he drew a magic circle around the cottage and told Sita not to step outside the ring: 'As long as you stay inside my circle you will be safe'.

Soon afterwards on old man came by. He asked Sita for help. She was a kind girl and did not want to refuse him so she stepped out of the circle. She did not know that this was the wicked Ravanna in disguise and that he had sent the deer to lure Lakshmana away and had then called out to Rama for help. Quickly Ravanna grabbed poor Sita and, changing into a giant bird, flew off with her to his island home of Lanka.

When Rama returned and found that Sita had been kidnapped he was heartbroken. He quickly vowed that he would rescue his wife and defeat Ravanna. Accompanied by his brother Laskhman, and with the help of Hanuman, the monkey king, he set out for Lanka. There they fought a fierce battle in which Rama was nearly killed and, after many adventures, they finally defeated the wicked Ravanna.

Sita was rescued and brought home. Everyone was delighted that the evil Ravanna had been destroyed and welcomed Rama and his beautiful wife with tiny lamps.

Because Hinduism is based on a non-European language some of the words have no exact translation, hence Diwali also appears as Divali, Dewali and Deepavali.

as the two festivals merge into one, with the deva lamps also being lit to welcome the return of Sita, it is usual to find the story told as part of the Diwali celebrations. The complete story is very long with many different elements to it. Below is the most popular part.

Festival activities

- Act out the story of Rama and Sita or use puppets to tell the story.

- Make deva lamps out of clay, playdough or Plasticine and use tea lights inside them.

- Colour in or draw your own rangoli patterns. These are usually symmetrical so you could make a stencil first by folding a circle into quarters and cutting out shapes, then opening it out and using it as a stencil or colour them in and use them as decorations. Alternatively, draw the pattern on card, spread it with glue and sprinkle with coloured rice powder or sand.

- Make diwali cards using images of Rama and Sita, Ganesh (the elephant headed god of good luck) or Lakshmi, goddess of wealth or devas and rangoli style patterns. Diwali cards are often bright and sparkly, so decorate with sequins and glitter.

- Make and enjoy Diwali sweets.

- Make New Year decorations with the words 'Sal Mubarak' (Happy New Year).

Christine Howard

Useful books

- *A Row of Lights – the story of Diwali* by Lynn Broadbent and John Logan (RMEP) (also available in big book format).
- *Diwali Story Big Book* by Anita Ganeri (Evans).
- *My Hindu Faith* by Anita Ganeri (Evans) (also available in big book format).

Useful artefacts and resources

- Rama and Sita Storytelling doll and book set; Diwali cards and lamps; and Ramayana Storybag from Articles of Faith, Suite 105, Imperial House, Hornby Street, Bury, BL9 5BN. Tel: 01992 454 636. Website: www.articlesoffaith.co.uk

Decorating for Diwali

Deva lamps

You will need: air-hardening clay, small candles or nightlights, clay tools.

Let the children handle the clay at first until it softens. It may help to have a small pot of water that they can dip a finger in and work into the clay. Form the clay into a small bowl shaped like a teardrop. Make a hole in the centre using a small candle or nightlight. Be careful that the base of the holder is flat so that it doesn't wobble! The surface of the clay can be decorated using clay tools. The children can scratch patterns into the clay or even push small dry pasta shapes into it. You might like to paint the finished lamp using brushes or spray paint.

You could paint pictures of deva lamps onto the windows using ready mix paint. If you add a drop of washing-up liquid to the paint it makes it easier to clean off later!

Rangoli patterns

These geometric patterns are made on the floors and doorsteps of houses to give thanks and make visitors feel welcome. During Diwali competitions are often held to design rangoli patterns. Traditionally they are made using coloured rice flour and follow elaborate designs that often include flowers. The rice flour also serves as food for wild birds, squirrels and even ants.

Try making your own pretty rangoli patterns. You can use lots of different materials such as seeds, rice, cereals, coconut, sand mixed with powder paint or food dye for colour. Make the patterns on strong pieces of card and place them on the floor or in the doorways. First apply glue in the required shape and then sprinkle the dry materials on top. The children could also make rangoli patterns using coloured chalks on an outside play area or pavement. You could have an exhibition of all the rangoli patterns.

Dressing up

At Diwali people enjoy wearing new clothes and decorating their hands and feet with mendhi patterns. Mendhi is made from henna and is a brown dye. Hindu brides also wear these traditional decorations. Ask children to draw around their hands on paper and design some mendhi patterns. Cut out the hand shapes and display them on the walls. Get children to experiment with making the mendhi patterns on their own hands and feet. They can use washable brown felt pen or paint and cotton wool buds. Can they make the patterns match? Is it easier to paint each others hands? How does it feel? Does it tickle?

Dancing

There are many dances associated with Diwali. One of the simplest to try with young children is the *dandia raas*. This uses *dandia* or decorated sticks.

You will need: 30cm lengths of dowelling, coloured sticky tape, paints.

Ask children to choose two different colours of tape or paint and decorate the sticks. Help children to find partners and stand facing one another. Can they tap the sticks together above their heads? Try tapping each others sticks. Ask children to turn around and tap the sticks together again. Can they dance around their partners? Try to find some Indian music for children to dance to or provide a simple drum beat. The dandia raas music starts slowly and gradually gets faster. Try inventing some simple moves of your own. As the music speeds up take care not to hit your partner's fingers by mistake!

Fireworks

Any Diwali party would not be complete without some fireworks. Remember the fireworks safety code and talk to children about keeping safe around fireworks.

Try making a group firework picture on black paper using fluorescent paints, glitter, silver and gold stars, and shiny paper. You can use toothbrushes to spray the paint effectively like sparks. Run your finger or thumb towards you, down the head of the toothbrush. (Try it the other way and you will get covered in paint!) Children will enjoy working together on a big painting to display on the wall.

Judith Harries

The Jewish festival of Hanukkah

Tell the story of Hanukkah and visit a place of worship to help bring the story alive. Visits to places of worship are one way of engaging children in an active exploration of the world in which they live. It is an opportunity for them to meet members of the community and learn, first hand, what a place of worship might look like.

It is important that children are properly prepared before a visit so that they understand what behaviour is expected of them. Parents and carers who are helping to supervise should also be carefully briefed beforehand.

You need to be clear about the aim of the visit, and whether you or a local religious person will speak with the children. Not all adults are able to talk to young children at their level, so this will need to be checked out, too.

The local church is often a good place to start as visits here are usually easy to arrange and within walking distance.

Once there, an effective approach is to encourage children to sit quietly, maybe close their eyes, listen to the stillness and experience the atmosphere of the place.

Many will have no experience of any place of worship. They may be overawed by its size, or the unfamiliar objects around them. Talk about how it feels and what they feel like. Think about why people come to a special place like this and link it with places that may be special to them.

Background to the festival

Hanukkah is a Jewish festival that commemorates the re-dedication of the temple in Jerusalem in 167 BCE. At this time Jewish worship was centred around the temple which was the focus for animal sacrifice and for the three pilgrim or 'foot' festivals: **Passover**; **Shavuot** and **Sukkot**.

Although Hanukkah is not one of the major festivals it is popular, probably because it takes place around the end

of December and, like Christmas, is associated with the giving of presents and the concept of light.

Antiochus Epiphanes was an ambitious Greek soldier. He conquered Israel and set about making the Jewish people like Greeks. He commanded them to stop keeping the Sabbath, studying the Torah, the Law which God had given them through Moses, and to stop worshipping their God and to worship him instead. He also forbade them to follow their dietary laws, amongst which was the prohibition of eating meat from pigs. The final insult came when he had a pig sacrificed in the temple, thereby making it unclean to the Jews.

In response to this treatment a group of Jews banded together under the leadership of Judas Maccabeus. They conducted a kind of guerrilla war against the Greeks and eventually overthrew them and drove them out of the temple. They then set about dedicating it afresh to the worship of God. How this happened is recorded in the Hanukkah story.

How to make and play dreidel

A dreidel is a four sided die or spinner. Each side has a Hebrew letter, said to represent the first letter of the words: 'A great miracle happened there.' Nes Gadol Haya Sham.

Nun  = do nothing

Heth  = take half

Gimmel  = get one

Shin ש = put one in

Each player has a number of counters. Each player rolls the die in turn and follows the instruction on the die. The winner is the one with all the counters.

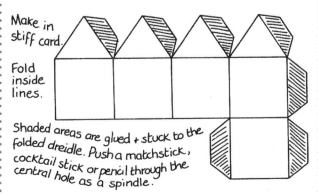

Make in stiff card.

Fold inside lines.

Shaded areas are glued + stuck to the folded dreidle. Push a matchstick, cocktail stick or pencil through the central hole as a spindle.

Recipe for latkes (serves 3-4)

Latkes are a traditional Jewish dish served at Hanukkah. They are fried in oil, a reminder of the oil that lasted eight days, enabling the Jewish people to rededicate the temple.

Ingredients
- 0.5 kilo potatoes, peeled and grated finely (2 baking potatoes)
- 1 egg, beaten
- 25g self-raising flour or matzah meal (1 tbsp)
- Salt and pepper to taste
- Olive or vegetable oil for frying.

Method
Squeeze the potatoes to get rid of excess water. Sieve the flour with the salt and pepper. Mix the flour, beaten egg and potato together. Take small handfuls of the mixture and shape into rounds about 1.5cm thick.

Heat the oil in a large frying pan. Add the potato rounds and fry until the underside is brown. Turn and brown on the other side. When cooked remove from pan and drain on kitchen towel.

Carry on until all the rounds are cooked. Serve hot.

Note: Oil can get very hot. It may be advisable for an adult to turn and fry the latkes.

For a quick and easy version why not try using instant potato instead of grated raw potato? Mix to a stiff consistency using less liquid than recommended.

This recipe can also be made substituting 1 cup of cooked, mashed cauliflower instead of the potato.

Finely chopped onion can be added to any of these recipes for added flavour.

Note on spellings and pronunciation

Because Hebrew is based on a different alphabet to English, some of the letters in Hebrew have no equivalent. Therefore, as with Sanskrit (the language of Hinduism) and Arabic (the language of Islam) there are alternative spellings, all of which are acceptable. For example Hanukkah and hanukiyah are sometimes spelt with a 'ch' at the beginning of the word. This is because the Hebrew 'h' is pronounced rather like the ch in 'loch' not like the 'ch' in chair.

The festival story

Abraham was reading the Torah with his granddaughter Miriam and grandson David when they heard soldiers coming. David and Miriam helped their grandfather hide the scroll and picked up some twigs for counters and a special dice from the cupboard. They started playing dreidel together.

Two soldiers entered the room. One looked over his shoulder and shouted: 'All clear here. It's only an old man and some kids playing some stupid game. Let's move on!' He turned away and they listened to the soldiers marching off.

'That was close,' said David, running to see where they had gone. Just then a man appeared from behind a bush where he had been hiding. 'Hello, David. Is your grandfather there?' he asked, entering the room.

David knew at once that this was the famous Jewish hero Judas, the Maccabean, who was a resistance fighter against the Greeks. Soon Judas was joined by other men. They had come to make a plan to fight the Greeks and drive them from the temple in Jerusalem. The two children were excited. They wished they could fight with them too.

It was just after dinner the next day that another visitor arrived. 'Have you heard the news?' the man shouted. 'Judas and his men have defeated the Greeks. We are free again. Once more we shall be able to worship in our temple.'

Abraham and the children quickly went up to Jerusalem to see what was happening there and to celebrate. They were surprised to see everyone looking very worried. What was wrong?

Grandfather went to find out and came back shaking his head.'We need to light the menorah to purify the temple and make it fit for worship but there is only enough of the special oil to keep it burning for one day. They have They have sent for more but it will take time for it to arrive.'

Every day for eight days David went to the temple with his grandfather. Every day they asked, 'Has the new oil arrived yet?' Every day they were told, 'No, but the menorah is still burning!'

Abraham shook his head in wonder. That one jar of oil lasted a full eight days until the new oil arrived and the temple was ready for worship again. A great miracle had happened.

This was the second Jewish temple, built in the time of Ezra and Nehemiah. The original temple had been built by Solomon, the king renowned for his wisdom. Herod the Great rebuilt the second temple but it was eventually destroyed in 70 CE by the Romans. One of the walls remains as the famous Western Wall.

Hanukkah is an eight-day festival. It is celebrated by the lighting of the hanukiyah. This is a nine-branched menorah or candelabra, sometimes called a Hanukkah menorah. One light is known as the servant or shemesh because it is used to light the other eight lights.

On the first night, one light is lit, on the second two and so on until all have been lit. This is because it was said that when the temple was re-dedicated there was only enough oil for one day but it lasted the full eight days until new oil was ready.

The hanukiyah is placed in the window so that passers by can see it and the lights are allowed to burn for at least half an hour. Special blessings are said at the lighting and often children will be encouraged to say these.

Cards and presents are exchanged and traditionally foods which use oil such as fried potato latkes or doughnuts are eaten.

According to tradition, playing the game of dreidel (pronounced dray-dul) was used to hide the fact that people were studying the Torah secretly, so dreidel is also played.

Festival activities
● Make a Hanukkah card.

● Make a dreidel and play.

● Build a model of the temple in Jerusalem.

● Make a hanukiyah from egg boxes or foil cups.

● Eat doughnuts or latkes.

Christine Howard

Useful books

● *Hanukkah Lights* (Chronicle) ISBN 978-0-81183-257-1

Useful artefacts and resources

● Model of Hanukkah temple
● A *hanukiyah*
● Dreidel.

Exploring Christmas traditions

Christianity is a multicultural religion with customs and practices which embrace cultures worldwide. Nowhere is this more apparent than in the celebration of Christmas.

Use Christmas as an opportunity to explore the diverse nature of Christianity by collecting examples of Christmas in different cultures. Christmas cards with greetings in a variety of languages and Christmas carols from various parts of the world are easy to find.

Posters and images of the Nativity seen through the eyes of different artists or crib sets from Africa and South America provide other examples. Many countries have their own Christmas stories such as the legend of the Poinsettia (South America) or Baboushka (Russia). The Gift Bearer, Santa Claus or Father Christmas is a tradition that appears in many forms depending on the part of the world it comes from.

Background
Our modern day image of Santa Claus owes its origins to the Americans and the Coca Cola Company in 1931. This

version, used to advertise their product, was probably based on an earlier depiction by Clement Clark Moore who wrote the poem 'A visit from St Nicholas' better known as 'The Night before Christmas'.

In this poem, Santa is described as a jolly elf who rides on a sleigh pulled by eight reindeer, visiting the homes of boys and girls to fill their stockings with presents. Thomas Nast, a famous cartoonist for *Harper's Weekly*, added to this image by presenting Santa with a fur trimmed suit and leather belt.

Santa actually arrived in America with Dutch settlers, who brought the tradition of Sinter Klaas, the Dutch version of Saint Nicholas, with them from their homeland. The red coat represented the red of his bishop's robe.

Saint Nicholas was the Bishop of Myra, in what is now Turkey. He was born in Patara, on the south coast of Turkey in the second half of the third century CE. Nicholas' parents were wealthy Christians, but they died from the plague when he was young and he inherited their wealth.

At the time Christians were persecuted and so he worshipped in secret. When Constantine became the Roman Emperor he converted to Christianity and the persecution of Christians ended.

Nicholas, who was a bishop by this time, became a man of authority and power. He was well known for his charitable works and the story of how he came to help a poor man, by anonymously giving him money, is at the root of the

Recipe: Christmas Lebkuchen

- 175g butter
- 450g sugar
- 10g cinnamon
- 1 teaspoon nutmeg
- 1 teaspoon grated lemon rind
- 225g dried peel (thinly sliced)
- 225g almonds, chopped
- 2 eggs, beaten well. 4 eggs yolks beaten well (save some of the white for glazing – use the rest to make meringues)
- 700g flour sifted with 2.5 teaspoons baking powder
- halved almonds for garnish.

Method
Turn on oven to 180 degrees, gas mark 4. Melt butter over low heat. Stir in sugar, spices, lemon, dried peel, chopped almonds and well-beaten eggs. Add flour and baking powder. Roll dough out thinly and cut into traditional Christmas shapes (stars and fir trees). Place half an almond in the centre of each biscuit, and brush the top of each biscuit with the white of an egg. Bake until brown.

Before planning extensive activities on a Christmas theme, check whether any families might have a religious objection. Further guidance on certain faiths, such as Jehovah's Witnesses and Islam, can be found in the relevant sections of this book. If in doubt, discuss it with parents.

The festival story

Meryem was so excited. Peter had asked her to marry him and she couldn't wait to share her news with her sisters, Havva and Canan. Breathlessly, she burst through the door of her house and danced around the room singing, 'I'm going to be married! I'm going to be married!' Havva and Canan laughed with her, but her father sadly shook his head.

'My darling daughter,' he said, 'How can you be married when I have no money for your dowry?'

In those days, girls could not get married without a gift of money from their father. This gift was called a dowry.

Meryem's father was very poor. They had scarcely enough money for food, so there was certainly nothing left for a dowry. That night Meryem cried herself to sleep.

Next morning she got up early and, with a sad heart, went to light the fire. There, in the hearth, was a bag of gold. Where had it come from?

Quickly she woke her sisters and father and together they looked at the unexpected gift. Suddenly Havva flung her arms around her sister.

'Meryem!' she cried with delight. 'Look! Now we have this money you can get married to Peter after all.' So soon Meryem was married.

Some time later, Havva met a young man she wanted to marry. Again, her father shook his head. He still had no money for a dowry.

That night Havva went to bed and cried herself to sleep. In the morning, when she came to light the fire, there in the hearth was another bag of gold. So, just like her sister, Meryem, she was able to marry. Still no-one knew where the bag of gold had come from.

Another year passed and it was Canan's turn to want to marry but her father still had no money. This time, however, Canan did not go to bed at all. Instead, she waited with her father to see if she, too, would receive a dowry from the unknown giver.

Late that night, a shadow appeared at the window and 'Thump!', a bag of gold landed on the hearth. Canan and her father rushed to the door and were just in time to see a figure dressed in a red cloak turning the corner.

Canan's father ran out shouting, 'Hey! Stop a moment!' The figure turned and the old man realised it was Nicholas, their bishop.

The father got down on his knees and grabbed hold of the bishop's red robe. 'Thank you, thank you, for everything you have done for me and my family,' he said.

Nicholas lifted the old man up. 'It's all right. It is right that I should share my wealth with those who have less than I. Just let's keep it our secret. That's all I ask,' and with that he turned and left for home.

His gift meant that Canan was able to get married, just as her sisters had done.

Saint Nicholas and his generosity are still remembered today, though you probably know him better as Santa Claus.

tradition of Santa Claus and his gifts of presents. He died in 340 CE on 6 December which is his feast day. In 1087 his bones were stolen by some sailors, who took them back to Bari on the east coast of Italy. They are kept there in the Basilica of St Nicholas and their arrival is still celebrated in Bari with fireworks every year.

Nicholas' fame spread throughout Europe via the Crusaders who visited Bari on their way to Jerusalem. In the twelfth century, French nuns, inspired by his story, secretly left presents of nuts, fruit and oranges at the houses of the poor, and so the practice spread.

Then during the Reformation in the 16th century, celebrations of St Nicholas were banned, so many of the festivities moved to Christmas Day.

In England, it is likely that Santa Claus became merged with a far older, pagan 'Father Christmas'. Victorian illustrations depict an elderly man with icicles or ivy around his head, and in some cases he wore a long green coat, rather than a red one.

St Nicholas is the patron saint of children, sailors, merchants and pawn brokers, which is why the symbol of the pawn broker is three gold balls, representing the bags of gold Nicholas gave to the poor man.

Festival activities
- Read the Christmas story – Christmas is a Christian, religious festival and the Nativity story lies at the heart of the celebration.

- Learn and sing Christmas carols from different countries.

- Use religious Christmas cards to make a frieze of the Christmas story.

- Read The Night before Christmas by Clement C Moore.

Christine Howard

Christmas around the world

Christmas or 'Christ's mass' is usually celebrated on 25 December and lasts for 12 days from Christmas Eve until Epiphany, 6 January. There are many stories and traditions associated with Christmas and each country has its own customs.

Giving
Present giving is an essential part of Christmas in all countries, originating from the story of the three wise men who brought gifts for the baby Jesus.

St Nicholas was a rich bishop living in the third century in Asia Minor, famous for his generosity. He is usually depicted as an old white-bearded man with a red cloak and mitre. In Holland, 5 December is Sinterklaas Eve and presents from St Nicholas are hidden throughout the house, with clues and poems teasing the person who should find them. The presents are wrapped in ingeniously shaped parcels or hidden inside things.

It is easy to see how Sinterklaas (the Dutch name for St Nicholas) became Santa Claus, who brings gifts to children in America and Britain. Father Christmas, too, derived from an old British legend, wears a long red coat, black boots and has a long white beard. His mode of travel in different countries varies from a sleigh pulled by reindeer or goats or an eight-footed horse (Scandinavia) to a surf boat (Australia).

Activity idea
Collect together as many different pictures of Santa Claus, in his various guises, from greetings cards, magazines, wrapping paper and ask children to cut them out and make a collage in the shape of a huge parcel or other Christmas shape. Talk about the different present giving traditions as you cut and stick.

Stories
In Russia there are many versions of the story of Baboushka who delivers presents to children on Christmas Eve. She is usually depicted as an old woman who one cold night was visited by the three wise men. They invited her to join them on their journey, following the star, but when she saw how cold it was she chose to stay in her warm home. The next day she changed her mind and tried to catch up with them, carrying a basket of presents for the baby Jesus, but there was no star in the sky for her to follow. So she still wanders the world searching, visiting each house at Christmas and leaving presents.

Italian children receive gifts at Epiphany (6 January) from a kind old witch called La Befana. Her name originates from young children's efforts to pronounce Epiphania! She was too busy cleaning her house when the wise men called by on their way to Bethlehem and she is forever wandering from house to house, looking for the new baby and leaving gifts just in case. Today she fills good children's stockings or shoes with presents, and leaves only coal for bad children.

On 5 January in Spain, people fill the streets for the Magi Kings' Parade. Children hope to deliver letters listing their present requests to the three kings as they ride by on their camels. That night Spanish children fill their shoes with straw and leave them out for the three kings. The camels eat the straw and leave presents in exchange.

Activity ideas
If you have any children in your group from other Christian European countries you could invite them and their families to visit you and share their first-hand experiences of these Christmas traditions. There are many picture books of Christmas stories from around the world. You could create your own book of stories using the children's own words, pictures and paintings.

Nativity scenes

The Nativity story has inspired many traditional customs and crafts. The first Christmas manger scene or *precipio* was life-sized, with real people and animals. St Francis of Assisi set it up in his tiny chapel in Italy more than 700 years ago. Nowadays, many town squares in Europe and America have Nativity scenes with figures of Mary, Joseph, baby Jesus, the shepherds and the three wise men.

Often people have miniature crib scenes made from wood or card in their homes. In Brazil, hand-made cribs or *presebres* are an important part of the family Christmas. Each member of the family is included alongside the usual Nativity characters and as the family grows new figures are carved and added to the scene.

Activity ideas

Using a simple keyhole shaped template and lots of suitable collage materials, try making your own nursery Nativity scene together. When you have made all the Nativity characters get each child to make a figure of themselves and mount them all on the wall under a large outline of a stable.

Traditions

Mexicans believe that Mary and Joseph's journey to Bethlehem took nine days.

Every night for the nine nights leading up to 24th December the people of the neighbourhood join together to form a posada. Four teenagers stand at the front of the procession carrying figures of Mary and Joseph. The group, each member holding a lighted candle, goes from house to house, seeking a place to stay. Outside each house they sing a simple carol requesting somewhere to stay. At the third house they are invited in and this is the place where the posada will stay for the night. First the group prays before the nativity scene which every home will have and songs and carols may be sung. Each night the posada ends with parties, music, fun and feasting. When the 24th December arrives every one goes to midnight mass and then home for a family dinner. There are no presents given on Christmas day itself as this is the day to concentrate on the birth of Jesus. Instead they have to wait until 6th January for the Day of the Kings (in Britain it is called the Feast of the Epiphany) before the children get their presents.

Activity idea

Have a doll dressed as Mary and Joseph and act out the posada by taking them to visit another classroom or divide the children into two groups so that one can be the posada and the other the hosts.

Alternatively, some groups might want to take the dolls home. This should be entirely voluntary and teachers should be aware of any areas of sensitivity that may arise eg when children of a non-Christian faith want to be involved. Send the dolls home with a journal or even a disposable camera so the child can record what the dolls did on their visit.

The children often play *piñata* during this time. Clay pots, shaped like animals and decorated in paper, are hung from the roofs. They are filled with water, confetti or sweets. The children stand in a circle around them and take it in turns to be blindfolded and, using a stick, try to break the *piñatas* – hoping to be showered with sweets and not water!

Activity idea

Try making *piñata* using balloons covered with several thin layers of *papier mache*. Cut the top off and remove the balloon. You could use paint or feathers to make them look more realistic. Fill them with confetti or perhaps raisins instead of sweets and replace the top. Suspend from the ceiling using ribbons at both ends and have fun trying to make them tip up. (There's no need to use a blindfold – some young children are nervous about this anyway.)

Decorations

Decorating homes and streets is a big part of most festivals and not least Christmas. The Christmas tree originates from Germany where it is decorated with gingerbread shapes and lighted candles. The fairy or angel on the top is the *Christkindl* (Christchild) who brings gifts to children on Christmas Eve.

In Finland, tiny candles shine in every window of the house. On Christmas Day, a straw framework is hung from the ceiling which the children decorate with coloured paper stars. Danish homes pride themselves in decorating their trees with completely home-made decorations. One favourite traditional shape is the heart.

Activity ideas

The children can try folding, cutting and weaving these hearts from red, green, gold and silver paper (see page 69). They can be hung on the tree with a sweet inside.

Add some mixed spice or ground ginger to a simple biscuit dough and make Swedish spice stars to hang on the tree. Don't forget to make a hole at the top of each star before baking! You can decorate them with coloured icing and silver balls.

Feasting

Christmas is always a time for special food and each country has its own traditional seasonal fare. In Norway, children bake 'thaw' biscuits, so called because the heat from thousands of ovens is supposed to melt the winter snow. In Holland a special cake called *Letterbanket* is eaten on

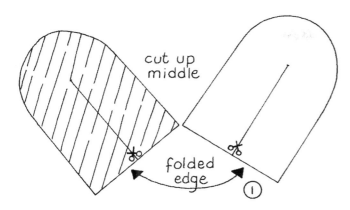

cut up
middle

folded
edge ①

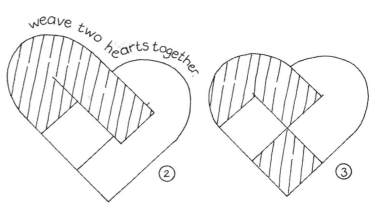

weave two hearts together

② ③

Christmas Eve. The pastry and marzipan mixture is shaped into the initials of every member of the family.

Activity idea
You could make a firm biscuit dough with children and help them to shape it into their initial letters.

In Poland, supper is served when the first star appears in the sky on Christmas Eve. A thin layer of hay is spread over the floor and under the tablecloth to remind people of the stable at Bethlehem. Before the meal a thin wafer of bread, an *oplatek*, with the Nativity scene imprinted on it, is passed around the table for each person to share. There are even places set for any absent friends or family members.

The traditional English Christmas pudding often contained money or charms to bring good luck to whoever found them. In Denmark, the traditional dessert is rice pudding. A single almond is hidden in the pudding and the person who finds it in their portion receives an extra present. The 'Crown of Kings' or Rosca de Reyes is a traditional Mexican sweet bread. It came from France and southern Spain and is eaten on the 6th January. Two tiny dolls are hidden in the dough representing the baby Jesus and a king. Whoever finds the baby becomes his godparent and together with the 'king' they host a party on Candlemas, (2nd February). This is the presentation of when Jesus in the Jerusalem temple took place and marks the end of the Christmas season. It is the role of the godparent to put the infant Jesus away until next Christmas.

Activity idea
Try making some bread dough with children. You could use a ready-mix bread dough for ease, although the traditional recipe is enriched with eggs and butter. Add 1 teaspoon each of cinnamon and mixed spice to the dry ingredients. Let the children watch the dough rise and talk about why this is. Include two small ceramic dolls in the dough. If these are not available two clean coins can be used instead. After the dough has proved (doubled in bulk) make it into a thick sausage and join the ends to make a circle. Brush with beaten egg and sugar. After baking decorate with crystallized oranges, candied fruit and glace cherries.

At Epiphany in both France and Spain a special kings' cake is served. The *Rosca de Reyes* is a large doughnut-shaped sweet loaf decorated with red, green and yellow glace cherries. It is baked with a coin or ring hidden inside and whoever discovers this is crowned 'King for the day'.

Activity idea
Try making some bread dough with children. You could either bake it as one large ring-shaped loaf or individual buns. Add a 10p coin to the dough before baking. Decorate the loaf with glace cherries and icing. On the last day of term you could share the kings' cake together. Help children to look out for the coin when they are eating so nobody hurts their teeth! Whoever finds the coin is king for the day and could have special privileges such as be first to have their snack, be first in the line or have their choice of activity, story or song.

Judith Harries

Useful books

- *This is the Star* by Joyce Dunbar (Doubleday) ISBN 978-0-55254-883-0. Simple but poetic retelling of the Nativity story accompanied by breathtaking oil paintings.
- *The Greatest Gift – The story of the other wise man* by Susan Summers (Barefoot Books) ISBN 978-1-84686-577-0. A retelling of the Victorian story of the fourth wise man's search for truth.
- *The first Christmas* by Jan Pienkowski ISBN 978-0-14150-097-3. Beautiful silhouettes with words from the King James Bible.
- *My very first Nativity Story* by Lois Rock ISBN 978-0-74596-911-4. Simple pictures and story for small children.
- *The Nativity Story* by Juliet David ISBN 978-1-85985-921-6. Colourful board book.

C is for Christmas

This idea for making stocking-shaped books, each one showing a letter from the word 'Christmas', encourages children to think about each letter and to make links between the letter shapes and their sounds.

They can draw upon a Christmas display for inspiration as they learn to identify words with the same initial sounds as the letters in the word 'Christmas'. Completing the books with pictures and words provides a resource for further written work.

Start by discussing with children what Christmas means to them. By exploring their understanding, you can help them to develop their vocabulary, ask questions and express their views and ideas with the group. Younger children may have only hazy recollections of previous Christmases, some may not celebrate this festival. Most will be aware that it is a time for giving presents, for decorating Christmas trees, and for hanging up stockings. Encourage children to contribute to a display of Christmas objects such as cards, baubles and wrapping paper and to bring in pictures relating to the theme for a wall display.

Christmas stocking books
Cut out nine large stocking-shaped book covers in bright sugar paper, and identically shaped sheets of white paper, in preparation for making books.

On each cover, draw in the outline of one of each of the letters in the word 'Christmas' and invite older children to use a contrasting crayon or felt pen to colour in the letters. Hang them in order in a row, at child height. Explain that the word formed by the stockings says 'Christmas'.

Linking sounds to letters
Each day, starting with the letter 'c', hold up one stocking in front of the children. Show them how to draw this letter in the air. Ask if anyone knows its sound, and encourage the others to repeat it as they practise its shape. Reinforce their understanding of this letter sound and its shape by making the shape in plasticine, painting it on large sheets of paper, drawing its outline in a tray of sand or cutting out pre-drawn shapes of the letter. Encourage children to refer to it frequently by its letter sound.

Repeat this activity with each of the other letters, returning each stocking to its place, to illustrate how together the sounds say 'Christmas'.

Finding words beginning with each letter sound

Use the display of objects and the wall display to help children identify Christmas words which begin with each letter on the stockings, such as cards, holly, reindeer. For example, start by asking, 'Can you find something which begins with the sound of c?' For 'i', suggest 'invitation' or 'igloo' but encourage children to think about different sounds 'i' makes in such words as 'icing'.

Younger children could also add their first names or the names of toys. Older children might widen the choice by adding winter words such as 'cold' or 'snow' or, depending on ability, you can include more abstract words such as 'merry' or 'happiness'.

Making and using the books
Concentrating on one letter at a time, invite children to fill the pages of each stocking book by cutting out and pasting in pictures of appropriate objects from catalogues and magazines, drawing small illustrations of their own or writing in the words using coloured pencils. Then staple on the covers. As the theme develops, and children suggest new words or ideas, make new pages. Children could choose different words from the books each day and use them to make up a class story together.

Ask older, or more able children, to draw pictures related to Christmas, or the created stories, and refer to the books to find appropriate words to use as they make up sentences for their own writing.

Other winter festivals
Discuss celebrations from other cultures which involve the giving of presents and sharing of special food – or invite children from other cultures to talk about their special days.

A Christmas alphabet

Before children can learn to read, they need to understand that the squiggles on a page, which we know as letters, mean something. This seasonal activity is a fun way of introducing children to the letters of the alphabet.

Look at the word 'Christmas' and talk about the sound that each letter in the word makes. Identifying a letter by its sound is the best way to help a child learn to recognise it.

For example:

cards holly reindeer

and so on.

You can use this Christmas tree as a kind of Advent calendar.

● Start by pointing at the bauble with the letter 'a' and talk about its sound.

● Then ask children to think of a word which begins with this letter sound, such as 'apple'. If they are unsure, give them some ideas, encouraging them to listen to beginning sounds in words.

● Once a word is chosen, let children colour in the bauble.

● Each day move to the next letter on the tree, until they are all completed.

Brenda Williams

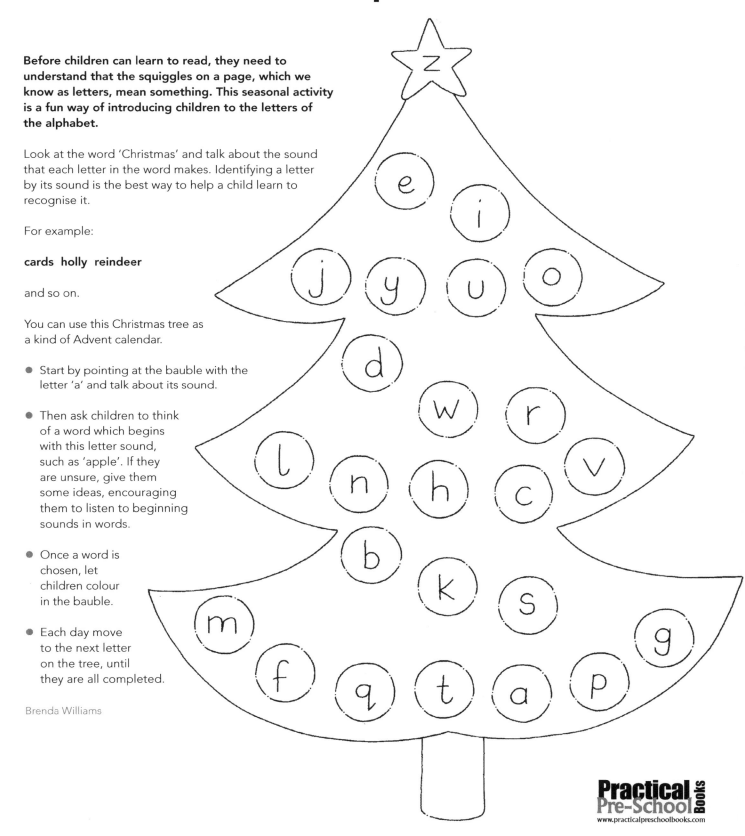

Practical Pre-School Books
www.practicalpreschoolbooks.com

Christmas craft

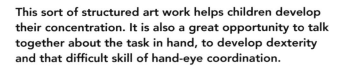

This sort of structured art work helps children develop their concentration. It is also a great opportunity to talk together about the task in hand, to develop dexterity and that difficult skill of hand-eye coordination.

Although everyone makes the same decoration, each child is able to express their creativity by choosing their own colours and printing blocks and making their own glitter trail. It is almost a group activity because everyone is following the same procedure and later groups can watch the pioneers do theirs. This does help develop a sense of community, encourages the timid ones and also helps children to feel that they are learning and growing like their friends.

Make a glittering stocking

This glittering stocking involves some simple printing. Have your own stocking ready made as an example and be prepared to do one with each group. Children can see what they are aiming for and can work with a sense of purpose. Yours can stay as decorations (maybe round a Christmas noticeboard) when children take theirs home.

You will need

Thin white card or good white cartridge paper; ready mixed paint in red and two shades of green; some things to print with (polystyrene shapes, sponge stars, cotton reels, tubes); flat containers for paint with a thick layer of foam in each; PVA glue and spreaders in small containers; silver glitter; cotton wool; red parcel ribbon.

Preparation

This activity is done in two stages, with the printing first and the dribbled glue second. You need a drying area for the printing or do the activity at two sessions.

Cut out the stocking shapes in advance to roughly A4 size. You could cut simple circles or diamonds so that those with other faiths can add them to their decorations. Prepare paints in trays and have bottles nearby to fill up as you go. Put only enough paint in the tray to be absorbed by the sponge so that the surface is not too wet. Choose printing items that have enough space for a good hand hold.

For the glue dribbling you need two separate ends of a large table, each with a large sheet of paper, one for the gluing and one for the glittering operation. Put the glitter in a saucer and after each child has finished pour the remaining glitter from the paper back onto the saucer.

The printing

Put each child's name on the back of their stocking before they start. Show children how to print by dipping the block into the paint, then scraping off any excess on the side of the tray. Place the printing block down gently to get a good image. Encourage them to make their own artistic choices – let them just use one colour and shape if they want, making any arrangement they like. Talk about the different shapes, sizes and colours and about what we use Christmas stockings for or about decorations in general. Let the paint dry thoroughly.

Glue dribbling

Put the painted stocking on the glue table and, using a glue spreader, take up a fair load of glue. Holding it about 30cm above the stocking, show children how to let the glue dribble in a spidery pattern over the paint. Move the spreader around to direct the glue. Young children are sometimes so fascinated by the dribble they forget to move the line around!

The glitter

Now move to the glitter area and put the stocking on the paper. The children can do all this themselves with a little guidance. Using their fingers, they need to pick up small piles of glitter and cover all the dribbles thickly, without touching the glue at all. Tip the stocking and tap it lightly to remove any excess and reveal the glittered lines over the bright paint. Save the remaining glitter before the next child comes.

Finishing off can be done by children on a different part of the table, but needs care if the glitter dribble is still wet. Glue cotton wool to the top edge of the stocking. When everything is dry, you can staple on a ribbon loop for hanging and add a greetings label on the back.

Rhona Whiteford

Planning a party

In early years settings December is usually dominated by activities based on the Christmas theme. A number of events take place which are organised by adults – but children can be involved in the planning, too.

Organising the Christmas party offers a range of learning opportunities. Introduce the party theme by talking about birthdays. Who has a birthday in December? What happens when it's your birthday? What happens at the party? Then talk about your forthcoming Christmas party and how they can be involved.

Writing and drawing

The party theme lends itself to lots of discussion and new vocabulary. There are also opportunities for writing and drawing. Provide some folded paper in the graphics area or writing table. Encourage children to draw a party picture on the front and 'write' an invitation to one of their friends. They could also make place names by writing their name on a card to indicate their seats. They could write a menu and draw the different foods they want for the party. The role-play area could be laid out as a party area.

Use fabric crayons on old sheets to make your own tablecloths. Provide plain white paper plates for children to decorate with pencil crayon. Encourage them to make their own party hats. Decorate the room with home-made Christmas decorations.

Involve children in preparing the food, making sandwiches and cakes, writing shopping lists. You could even take a group out shopping for the food. On the day of the party, sit children in small groups and talk about how many plates they need, how many cups and so on. Develop personal and social skills by choosing one person from each table to be the waiter or waitress and give out the party food and drink. Older groups can have a jug on the table and pour their own drinks. Encourage children to clear away their own litter by providing each table with a litter bin or bag.

Children could create table decorations by spraying fir cones with gold and silver paint, or making snowmen from cardboard tubes and cotton wool. Place Christmas evergreens such as holly, ivy, mistletoe or a poinsettia plant in the middle of each table.

Sing to Santa

If you have a visit from Father Christmas make sure children know in advance and be prepared for some children to be

Mince pies

- 200g puff pastry
- 200g mincemeat.

Method
Roll out the puff pastry approximately 2mm thick. Cut half of the pastry into fluted circles (about 5cm in diameter). Place on a greased baking sheet. Place a teaspoon of mincemeat in the middle of each circle. Moisten the edges. Cut the remainder of the pastry into slightly larger rounds (6cm in diameter). Cover the mincemeat and seal the edges. Brush with beaten egg.

Bake in a hot oven (240 degrees) for 20 minutes. Allow to cool. Sprinkle with icing sugar.

upset. Ring some sleigh bells and warn them that he is on his way. If possible, get him to wave through the window on his way into the building. When he arrives, sit him down and get children to sing him some songs. This will give them the time they need to adjust to his presence and then, of course, he can give out the presents.

Party games

The old favourites are the most successful but need adapting for the age group. In 'Pass the parcel', for example, instead of sitting in one large group, divide children into smaller circles so they are not waiting as long and more get a turn at opening the parcel. Put a small gift in each layer so they all have something rather than leaving it for the last child and having a lot of other disappointed children.

Children enjoy 'Musical statues' but some do not really understand the rules. Avoid having children 'out' sitting for any length of time. Let them stay in but just play 'dance and stop'. Say you are looking for the best dancer and give a small prize to one boy and one girl. Don't force children to join in. If they prefer to watch, just provide something for them to play with in a corner.

After the party food and games are over, sit children down for a Christmas story or to sing some Christmas songs. Choose some to help with the tidying up.

Caroline Jones

Good News!
– a nursery Nativity

Cast list:

- Narrator – this should be an adult
- Angels
- Mary
- Joseph
- Donkey
- Soldiers
- Shepherds
- Innkeeper
- Innkeeper's wife
- Star
- Chorus.

This Nativity has been specially written for young children. It uses simple language and the songs can all be sung to traditional tunes.

Character(s): **Stage directions**
Children in places. Angels standing.
Mary sitting looks towards angels.
Music group – metal instruments.

Narrator: Our story begins when angels visit Mary and give her some very good news.

Angels: You're having a baby, a fine baby boy,
He'll be very special, he'll bring you great joy.

Narrator: But Mary was frightened.

Mary: How can this be, please tell me some more,
I don't understand, I'm not very sure.

Narrator: So the angels explained …

Angels: Your baby's from God, it's really good news,
You'll call him Jesus, he'll be King of the Jews.

Angels sit.

Narrator: Mary was still not very sure, so her husband, Joseph, said:

Joseph stands.

Joseph: I'm Joseph, a carpenter, I make things from wood.

Music group – wooden sounds.

Don't worry Mary, I'm sure he'll be good.

Joseph sits. Chorus stands. Voice/piano/tape intro.

Chorus: Song 1: 'Good News'.

Narrator: Soon Mary and Joseph had to set off on the long journey to Bethlehem where they would be counted.

Their trusty donkey would help them get there.

Donkey stands – mask on.

Donkey: I am the donkey for Mary to ride, She's having a baby and gets very tired.

Chorus: Song 2: 'Trusty Donkey'.

Mary and Joseph stand.

Narrator: After a long, tiring journey they reached Bethlehem and Joseph said:

Chorus sits.

Joseph: We'll go and be counted, I'm sure it's this way,
And then I'll find somewhere for us to stay.

Mary, Joseph and Donkey sit.

Narrator: They found the place where soldiers were counting people as they passed.

Soldiers stand.

Soldiers: We are the soldiers who count all these folk,
One, two, three, four, five – it's really no joke!

Chorus stands.

Chorus: Song 3: 'One, two, three, four, five'.

Chorus and soldiers sit.

Narrator: As it was getting dark, they needed somewhere to stay.

They knocked on many doors but each innkeeper said,

'No room here'. All except one.

Music group – five wooden knocks, five children in Chorus say in turn 'No room here'.

Innkeeper and wife stand.

Innkeeper: I am the innkeeper, no room at all, Except for a stable and a cattle stall.

Narrator: Then the innkeeper's wife said to Mary and Joseph:

Innkeeper's wife: If you'd like to stay there, I'll fetch some more hay, It's lovely and soft, I'll show you the way.

Innkeeper's wife points to side of stage. Innkeeper and his wife sit.

Chorus stands.

Chorus: Song 4: 'A baby so special'.

Chorus sits, animal masks on.

Narrator: It sounds as if Mary and Joseph and baby Jesus were not alone in the stable.

Animal noises.

Animals: We are the animals, camels, sheep and cows, The stable's our home but we're sharing it now.

Animals sit, masks on floor.

Narrator: The stable was quite full already.

Angels stand.

Suddenly, some angels appeared in a bright light. They told the shepherds about baby Jesus.

Shepherds kneel up and shield their eyes.

Shepherds: Wow!

Narrator: said the shepherds sat round their camp fire, That light's so bright it is hurting our eyes.

Narrator: And the angels said:

Angels: Get up lazy-bones, don't lie around:

Chorus and star stand.

Take your sheep to Bethlehem town.

Angels sit.

Chorus: Song 5: 'Wake up, Wake up!'

Chorus points at star then sits.

Narrator: And sure enough, in the night sky was a beautiful bright star shining right over the stable where Jesus lay.

Star: I am the star in the East so bright, There's good news for all on this Christmas night.

Chorus stands.

Chorus: Song 6: 'Holy star'.

Chorus sits.

Narrator: The star shone so brightly that three wise men a long way away saw it and decided to follow it. It led them all the way to baby Jesus and they gave Him presents.

Wise men stand holding gifts.

Wise Men: We've brought Jesus some presents from lands afar, There's frankincense, gold and myrrh in a jar.

Each wise man says own gift.

Chorus: Song 7: 'Three wise men'.

Narrator: And so everyone knew that Jesus was a very special baby. And although it happened a long time ago, He still lives in our hearts today.

Everyone stands.

All: Reprise: Song 6: 'Holy star'.

Children: Happy Christmas!

Song 1: Good News!
Words: Peter Morrell Tune:Traditional

We hear good news, We hear good news, From the An - gels, From the An - gels, Good news, Good news, Ba - by Je - sus is near.

Song 2: Trusty Donkey
Peter Morrell

Trust - y don - key, Trust - y don - key, car - ry Ma - ry safe - ly. Trust - y don - key, Trust - y don - key, Safe to Beth - le - hem.

Song 3: One, two, three, four, five
Words: Peter Morrell Tune: Traditional

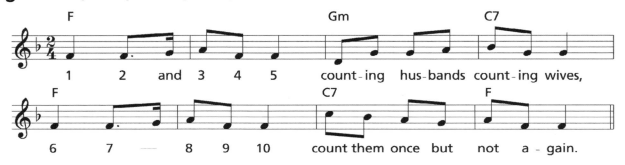

1 2 and 3 4 5 count - ing hus - bands count - ing wives, 6 7 8 9 10 count them once but not a - gain.

Song 4: A Baby so Special
Words: Peter Morrell Tune: Traditional

So Ma - ry and _ Jo - seph had _ some-where to stay. And the ba - by was born and He __ slept on the hay. ba - by so __ spec - ial ly - ing there in the night. And _ all round the sta - ble was a won - der - ful light.

Song 5: Wake Up, Wake Up!

Words: Peter Morrell Tune: Traditional

Wake up, Wake up, all you wool-ly sheep. Off to Beth-le-hem you must creep.

Off you go it is-n't ve-ry far, Off you go and fol-low that bright star.

Song 6: Holy Star

Words: Peter Morrell Tune: Traditional

Twin-kle, twin-kle, ho-ly star, Shin-ing bright-ly from a-far.

Up a-bove the cat-tle stall, Bring-ing good news to us all,

Twin-kle, twin-kle, ho-ly star, Shine for-ev-er where we are.

Song 7: Three Wise Men

Words: Peter Morrell Tune: Traditional

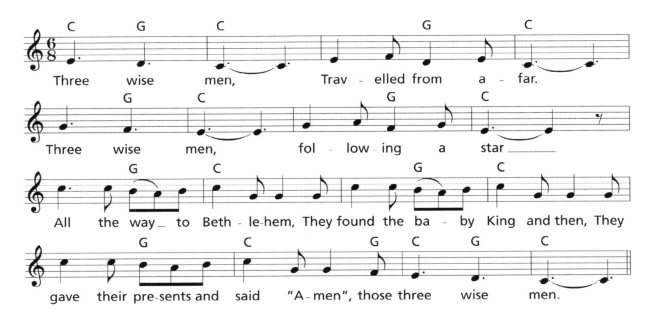

Three wise men, Trav-elled from a-far.

Three wise men, fol-low-ing a star

All the way to Beth-le-hem, They found the ba-by King and then, They

gave their pre-sents and said "A-men", those three wise men.

Performing the Nativity

The set

The set can be as simple or as complex as you want and will largely depend on the setting you are in. The performance can be staged successfully without any set at all. Try to acquire safe, sturdy boxes/blocks/ small benches/low tables/chests, which will help to create different levels for the Angels, Star and Mary and Joseph. This also helps the audience.

Scenery

Again, this depends on your setting and how many parents you can enlist to help – and how good they are with a paintbrush! If you have time, try creating:

● Paper shapes (palm trees, silhouette houses, stable scene) cut from sugar paper and fixed behind the set.

● A draped background with a scene painted on large sheets and hung from a rail or rod.

● If medical screens are available, background scenery can be draped over them, or simply drape a piece of material over them – blue is effective.

● A collage of children's paintings about the story.

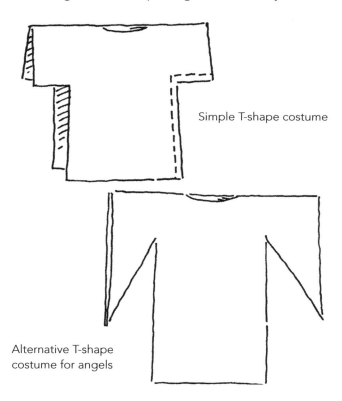

Simple T-shape costume

Alternative T-shape costume for angels

Costumes

Keep costumes simple, although it is important for children to have some items to dress up in as it helps them to take on a different role.

Put out an appeal for old sheets in good time or send a pattern home to willing parents. White or pastel colours are effective. You can base all the costumes on a simple T-shape pattern using a single piece of material folded at the neck. Tie a piece of string, thin rope or dressing gown cord round the middle to give it shape. Check the neck opening allows the head to go through! In this way, you should avoid the situation whereby some children have incredible costumes, the result of hours spent by parents labouring over a sewing machine – and others have nothing.

Angels: add tinsel/lametta to costume and around a headband. (See left for alternative T-shape for angel costume.)

Mary: add a blue cloak with a rectangle of white material over the head secured with a simply decorated headband. Joseph, Shepherds, Innkeepers: T-shape could be in striped or slightly coarser material (check the itch factor!)

Three Wise Men: add items to give the effect of wealth – bangles, brooches, old necklaces. Headgear should denote wealth.

Star: add shaped headband with silver/gold stars.

Animals: make masks from a basic design and attach features such as ears and nose, and colouring of the animal. There are camels, sheep, cows and, of course, the donkey in the script, but other animals (farmyard type) could appear. Cereal box card would be adequate. Either attach a piece of elastic to secure it to the head or tape a ruler (or similar) to the back of the mask so that each animal can hold the mask in front of their face. Remember eye-holes and name! A jumper, T-shirt or similar in the animal's colouring would help the mask to blend in.

Props
Keep props to a minimum.

- **Manger:** a cardboard box covered/painted brown, straw or material, baby Jesus (suitable doll) swaddled in a piece of white material, small stool/table for box to rest on.

- **Presents:** frankincense – a small urn/ interesting shaped container; gold – chocolate box wrapped in gold paper or spray painted; myrrh – dark coloured jar or similar (not glass!)

- **Shepherd's crook:** length of beanpole (made to measure) with a shaped wire head bound in brown sticky tape.

- **Star:** a five-point star of card, covered in silver paper and suspended above the manger.

- **Large story book:** for the narrator.

Music
There are seven short songs and their aim is to reinforce the story. Don't worry if you don't have a piano – just start singing!

With the exception of Song 2, 'Trusty Donkey', all the songs are based on traditional tunes which should be familiar to most children – and all adults, hopefully.

All the songs are within the children's pitch range and contain phrases that go in small steps (Song 2) as well as ones that move in larger intervals (Songs 1 and 5). There are a variety of rhythms and key signatures to give further musical experience.

Chord symbols have been added above the music and can be used by a pianist (to fill out the melody line) and/or a guitarist.

Song 1: 'Good News!'
The tune is based on 'London's Burning' and when it is fully learned, try two-part singing. Group 1 sings through twice; Group 2 starts when Group 1 reaches * and sings through twice, finishing two bars after Group 1. The music group can play the rhythm 'Good news' on the first and second beats of each bar.

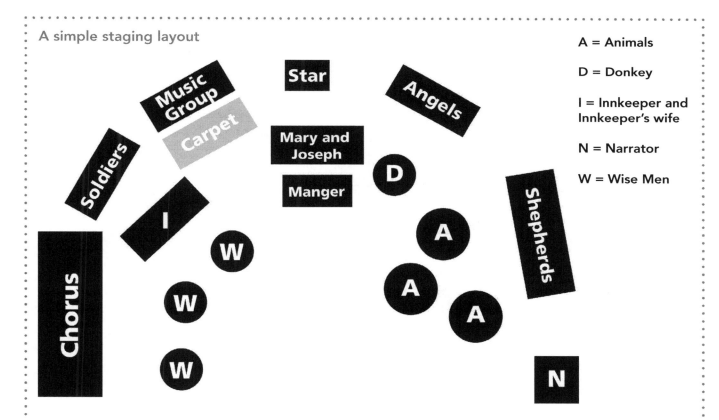

A simple staging layout

A = Animals

D = Donkey

I = Innkeeper and Innkeeper's wife

N = Narrator

W = Wise Men

The children can be in their places throughout the performance, and stand when speaking/singing. This will give a tableau effect when they are in costume. Angels and Star can be on a raised level, safe enough to stand on. Mary and Joseph sit on raised level. Other characters/chorus sit on floor. Position adult helpers with each group.

Song 2: 'Trusty Donkey'

The tune progresses in gentle steps and the music group can play wooden instruments (coconut shells are good for donkey sounds) in a walking pace to don – key, don – key.

Song 3: 'One, Two, Three, Four, Five'

This is based on the tune to 'Once I caught a fish alive'. The Music Group can accompany with the rhythm one, two, three, four, five. Played four times.

Song 4: 'A Baby so Special'

This uses the tune for 'Away in a manger'. The triangle (or similar) in the music group could play softly on the first beat of each bar.

Song 5: 'Wake Up, Wake Up!'

The tune is, of course, 'Baa Baa Black Sheep'. The music group can play to the words 'Wake Up' in each bar.

Song 6: 'Holy Star'

Sung to the tune 'Twinkle, Twinkle, Little Star'. If you have or can acquire a glockenspiel, one child in the music group can very lightly run up and down the bars with the beater during the first two lines and the last two lines, to give a twinkling effect.

Song 7: 'Three Wise Men'

This is sung to the tune 'Three Blind Mice'.

'Holy Star' can be sung by everyone, including the audience, at the end.

Rehearsals

Don't let them dominate your life. Remember, over-rehearsing can take the fun out of the whole event. Incorporate the performance into other activities – art, movement, music sessions. The songs can be introduced during music sessions with the whole group and movement incorporated when learned.

Involve your parents from the beginning so that they understand the project and can hopefully support it in a practical way. The song-sheet can be photocopied to give to parents for them to sing with their child(ren) at home. The script may also photocopied.

Music group

A small group of children can add rhythm and sound effects to the performance. Put a mat (or similar) on the floor in front of them and insist that when the instruments are not being played they must rest on the mat. This will develop good practice.

Have three types of instruments – wooden (rhythm sticks, guiros, Chinese blocks); shaker (yogurt pots with beads/rice/peas, cardboard rolls with same contents, maracas); metal (tubes like those in wind chimes, triangle, glockenspiel – see Song 6). Some of these could be made in activity sessions.

In preparation time, play games like 'guess the sound' where you play an instrument but the children cannot see you and they try to guess which instrument made the sound. 'Simon says play the... ' is effective for children to recognise instruments by their proper name. Show children how different instruments can be played and how the same instrument can make different sounds depending on how it is played. Explain how precious the instruments are and that they must be looked after.

There are opportunities for the music group to compose sound effects for the performance. Such as:

- Whole group rhythm patterns at the beginning;

- Metallic sounds when the angels stand/sit;

- Wooden sounds when Joseph says, 'I make things from wood';

- Wooden sounds for knocking on the inn doors – synchronisation could be interesting!

- Shaking sounds for the hay;

- Shaking/metallic sounds for the shining star.

The Muslim festival of Muhammad's birthday

Some Muslims do not celebrate the birthday of Prophet Muhammad (pbuh) but those who do will sing songs and tell stories of his life. We relate some of those stories in a form that young children will understand and enjoy.

Islam, like most of the world faiths apart from Western Christianity, does not follow the Western, solar based, calendar. Its years are dated from the Hijrah, the flight from Makkah (or Mecca) which took place in 622 CE.

The suffix used in Islamic year dating is AH, which refers to the Hijrah, rather than AD, Anno Domini, standing for 'In the year of Our Lord' (Christian) or CE, Common Era (equivalent to AD but felt to be more appropriate in a multifaith society).

The Hijrah was a critical event in the development of Islam and marks the time when Muhammad and his followers left their home in Makkah in fear for their lives. They set up a community in Madinah (Medina), a city 200 miles north of Makkah. This is where the first mosque, outside of the Kab'ah in Makkah, was built and where the Prophet Muhammad is buried.

The Muslim calendar is based on the phases of the moon. This lunar calendar is shorter than the solar one being only 354.36 days long (12 x 29.53). As a result of this the dates of festivals alter each year relative to the Western calendar, cycling back by about 11 days.

Muhammad's birth day was 20 August 570 CE which fell on the twelfth day of Rabi' al-awwal, the third month of the Muslim calendar.

Background

The Prophet Muhammad's birthday, Milad-un-Nabi, may be marked in a similar way to other Islamic festivals with food being shared with family and friends. However, celebrations are muted because the Prophet's death is also remembered, as this is believed to have happened in the same month.

Some Muslims do not celebrate at all, claiming that there is no evidence that Muhammad celebrated birthdays and/or that he did not want Muslims to mark his birthday in the way that Christians celebrate the birth of Christ.

The initials placed after the Prophet's name (pbuh) stand for 'peace be upon him'. They are a mark of respect. Sometimes the letters SAW are used, standing for 'peace and blessings be upon him' in Arabic, or it can be written in Arabic.

Representations of the Prophet Muhammad (pbuh)

Islam, like Judaism, forbids the making of 'graven images'. In modern Islam this extends to representations of the prophets, including the Prophet Muhammad.

It is important to remember this when working with young children, so that offence is not inadvertently given to the community by children drawing pictures of Muhammad or by role-playing his character in drama. Instead use artwork as an opportunity to explore the wonderful geometric designs, mosaics and tessellations that are characteristic of Islamic art and architecture.

Check all resources to make sure they do not contain representations of the Prophet. If they do, it suggests that the author/editors are ignorant of some fundamental aspects of Islam and this should lead you to question the accuracy of the rest of the work.

It is interesting, however, that such prohibitions were not in place in medieval times. It is possible to see paintings of the prophets in art work from this period though sometimes they appear with the faces blanked out.

Where there are celebrations, they focus on the life and teachings of Muhammad and in particular on remembering how he forgave even the worst of his enemies. It is customary to have communal gatherings where the preacher concentrates on Muhammad's teachings and special prayers are said. Gifts are given to the poor. In the home, parents sing songs about Muhammad and tell stories of his life.

The festival story

Prophet Muhammad (pbuh) was not happy. He had been told by Allah (God in Arabic) to preach in his home city. He had told the people how it was wrong to make and sell statues of different gods. He had told them there was only one God, Allah, and that He was the God they should all be praying to. Time and again he had repeated the words: 'La ilaha Illa Allah. There is only one God.' The Prophet was upset because the people wouldn't listen to him. In fact, they threatened to kill him and his Friends. He had to get away – quickly.

So he left Makkah secretly and hurried away into the desert, north of the city. However, he was still not safe. When the men of the city found that he had escaped, they were angry and set out to find him and kill him. Up in the hills, Muhammad could see a band of fierce men tracking him, getting closer and closer. What was he to do?

Muhammad did the best thing he could. He prayed to Allah for help. 'Please keep me safe, Insha'Allah, God willing'

Just then Muhammad saw a cave nearby and it seemed to him that Allah was telling him to hide in it. It was dark and cold in the cave and Muhammad was sure that the men would find him, as the entrance to the cave was wide and unhidden. Crouched at the back of the cave he could hear the men's voices getting nearer. Then a loud voice shouted, 'Look, over here. There's a cave. He could be hiding in there.' Muhammad could hear more voices muttering at the entrance to the cave. The bodies of the men cut out all the light from the place where he was hiding, and he was sure that any moment they would come and seize him. He held his breath, shut his eyes tightly and continued to pray: 'Please keep me safe, Insha'Allah, God willing.'

Eventually, Muhammad heard the men move away from the cave. He was safe. Relieved, but puzzled, Muhammad carefully crept to the entrance of the cave to peer out. Something cool and tickly brushed against his face. It was a spider's web and above it he saw a nest with a dove, cooing gently. Muhammad put his hand up to wipe it away but stopped suddenly. Now he knew what this meant. Allah had sent a spider to spin a web across the face of the cave and the dove to nest there. When the men had seen them they had turned away because they thought that no-one could have entered the cave without disturbing the web and the dove.

So Allah saved his Prophet from the evil men and Muhammad was able to continue his journey to Madinah. Here he and his followers built a new mosque and worshipped Allah faithfully for the rest of their lives.

Muhammad's father, Abdullah, died before Muhammad was born. By the time he was eight years old both his mother, Aminah, and his grandfather had died so he was brought up in the home of his uncle, Abu-Talib.

He worked first as a shepherd boy and then accompanied his uncle on a caravan trip across the Arabian peninsula where he came into contact with Jewish and Christian communities. By the age of 25 he was a merchant for a wealthy widow Khadijah, whom he eventually married. She was to become a great support and comfort to him.

Muhammad was 40 when he received the first of many revelations from Allah. He felt that Allah wanted him to preach to the people of Makkah, who worshipped many strange idols. However, his message was resented, because it threatened the livelihoods of the corrupt idol makers of the city. They were determined to kill Muhammad, but he learned of the plot, left Makkah secretly and escaped from them to Madinah. He joined his followers, many of whom had already emigrated there and made it his home.

Festival activities

- Learn and sing some Muslim nursery rhymes.

- Make and decorate tessellations and geometric patterns. Use them to decorate a card for someone special.

- Look at pictures of the Kab'ah in Makkah and Prophet's Mosque in Madinah. Learn more about/visit mosques.

- Look up Saudi Arabia in an atlas and find Makkah and Madinah.

Christine Howard

Recipe for chapattis (makes about 20)

Traditional Indian/Pakistani unleavened bread recipe.

Ingredients
- 450g chapatti or wheat flour
- 2 tbsp cooking oil.

Method
Mix the flour and oil by hand in a mixing bowl, slowly adding enough hot water (approx 350ml) to make a soft dough. Knead for a few minutes and then leave to rest for around 20 mins. Divide the dough into small balls. Roll them into round, flat circles on a floured board. Cook on a griddle for 20-30 seconds, then turn over and cook the other side. Traditional chapattis are finished by moving them around in a naked flame for a few seconds until they puff up. You can grill them for a few seconds instead. They are delicious served with butter but can be eaten without.

The Muslim festival of Eid ul-Fitr

Most major world faiths have special or sacred books and for Muslims this is the Qur'an. The giving of the Qur'an is remembered during Ramadan which ends with the celebration known as Eid ul-Fitr.

Sacred books are important for all the major world faiths. They are the means by which the beliefs and faith of the religion are handed down from generation to generation.

However, the way these sacred writings are regarded vary between religions and even within religions. One example of this, taken from Christianity, is the story of creation in Genesis (from the Old Testament part of the Bible). Some Christians look upon this as mythology, a way of describing a divine truth that God created the world and everything in it, but not to be taken literally as a scientific account. Others regard the Bible as literal truth. Where science would appear to differ from that account, they claim that this is a test of faith. Similar views of scripture can be found in other religions, too.

Whatever your personal feelings are on these points, you need to recognise that sacred writings are of great importance to the believer and should be treated with respect, both in the way that you handle the books themselves, should you have them in your care, and in the way that you talk about them and their contents.

Muslims, the name for those who follow the religion of Islam, regard the Arabic **Qur'an**, their scriptures, as the actual words of Allah (God). Because of this they treat the book itself with great respect. They wash their hands before handling it, keep it on a stand, do not put anything above it other than religious posters or pictures, and keep it covered when not in use. Menstruating women are forbidden to handle it at all.

If you decide to keep a Qur'an in your classroom, it is advisable to follow the same rules as a Muslim would, when handling or storing it. This not only avoids causing any offence, it is also a dramatic visual aid for young children, who can see that this is a special book by the way in which it is handled. However, try to make it clear to them that the way that it is handled is because it is special since Muslims believe it is the Word of God. It is not the handling that makes it special.

Background

The name Qur'an means 'recite'. It is the name given to the Muslim holy book because, according to Muslim belief, this is what the Angel Jibrael (Gabriel) told Muhammad to do.

Recipe for *Wedhmi*: a traditional Eid dish

Pastry
- 4oz self-raising flour
- pinch of salt
- 4oz margarine or butter
- cold water to mix.

Filling
- 8oz dessicated coconut soaked in water for 30 mins and drained
- 4 tbsp sugar
- cardamon seed
- stick of cinnamon.

Pre-heat the oven to 200 C; Gas mark 6.

Method
To make the pastry: Sift the flour and salt together. Cut the fat into small cubes. Rub fat into flour between fingers and thumb until it is like breadcrumbs. Mix to a stiff dough with cold water.

To make the filling: Mix the ingredients together. Fry them in melted margarine or butter. Roll out pastry and cut out rounds using pastry cutter. Place a small amount of filling on the pastry round and fold in half. Damp the edges with a drop of water and press down. Bake in a hot oven for 15 minutes.

The festival story

Muhammad was sad. The people in his home town of Makkah prayed to statues of gods and would not listen to him when he told them that there was only one God, Allah, and that they should pray to Him alone. He climbed up into the mountains where he often went to be alone and to think.

While he was there, he suddenly felt that there was someone else with him. He looked up and there, standing in front of him, was a man dressed in white. It was Allah's special messenger, the angel Jibrael, which you may know as Gabriel.

Muhammad was speechless. He didn't know what to do or say, but the angel spoke to him and told him not to be afraid. 'I have a special job for you,' he said. 'Allah has sent me to give you a message for his people. You must write down what I tell you.'

Muhammad did not know what to say.

'I can't do that,' he muttered. 'I don't know how to write.' In those days lots of people couldn't read or write. But the angel insisted. 'Recite,' he said, 'In the name of Allah, who creates man from a clot of blood'.

Muhammad shook his head again, but the angel kept on insisting until Muhammad gave up and agreed to do what the angel had demanded.

Later that day he returned home. He was confused and worried about what he had been told to do. He told his wife Khadijah all that had happened. She was a sensible woman and she knew straightaway that it was Allah asking Muhammad to do this difficult thing. She told him that she was sure that everything would be all right and that Muhammad could do it, inshallah (which means 'if Allah wants it').

So Muhammad began to write down the words that the angel had given him from Allah. This is the very first word that he wrote: Bismillah – in the name of Allah.

Over the months he kept going back up into the mountain and the angel would keep coming to him and giving him more to write down, until eventually he had completed the words of Allah in the book which is now called the Qur'an, a word that means 'recite', because that is what the angel told Muhammad to do.

Today all Muslim children are encouraged to go to a special school called the Madrassah where they learn the Qur'an in Arabic, the language that Muhammad wrote in.

The Qur'an was revealed to Muhammad over a period of time. It is divided into 114 chapters, called surahs, arranged by length with the shortest surahs first. Each surah has a title taken from something that appears within the chapter.

The Qur'an is not an easy book for young children and you will not find Qur'anic stories for children in the way that there are versions of the Bible to read to this age group. However, there are stories of the Prophets and other well-known Muslim stories for young children.

The giving of the Qur'an is remembered during the fast month of Ramadan on the Lailat ul Qadr or Night of Power. On this night Muslims will read through the whole of the Qur'an in Arabic.

Ramadan is a month when Muslims abstain from all food and drink between the hours of sunrise and sunset. It is one of the five pillars or duties of Islam which all Muslims try to follow. In hot countries and in the UK during the summer when the days are long, this can be very difficult. Children who have not reached puberty are not required to fast although they may start to learn the discipline by going without sweets or other treats. Anyone who is ill, and pregnant or nursing mothers are not expected to fast.

At the end of Ramadan a special celebration is held known as **Eid (or Id) ul-Fitr** or Little Eid (as opposed to Eid ul-Adha which is the celebration at the completion of the Hajj, pilgrimage to Makkah).

At this time new clothes are bought, cards and presents exchanged and special meals prepared. Special Eid prayers are recited at the mosque and a greeting, 'Eid Mubarak' meaning 'a blessed Eid' is shared. It is also customary to give to the poor at this time.

Some books, and indeed some Muslims, speak of Eid as a Muslim Christmas. This is misleading and should be discouraged. Elements of each celebration may be similar, such as the giving and receiving of presents and cards, but for Christians, Christmas is the celebration of the birth of Jesus Christ, God incarnate, whereas Eid is the celebration of the end of a month long fast.

Festival activities

● Make an Eid card or Eid sweets.

● Listen to a small part of the call to prayer or a reading from the Qur'an in Arabic.

● Try drawing mosques or colouring in some geometric patterns.

Christine Howard

Eid ul-Adha (Great Eid)

The other important festival in the Muslim calendar is Eid ul-Adha or Great Eid. Eid ul-Adha is the festival that takes place at the end of the Hajj. It lasts between one and three days.

Background to the festival
Every Muslim is required to observe five duties, usually known as the Five Pillars of Islam. They are:

1 **The declaration of faith** – 'There is no God but Allah and Muhammad (pbuh) is His prophet'

2 Prayer five times a day **(Salat)**

3 Giving to Charity **(Zakat)**

4 Fasting during the month of Ramadan **(Sawm)**

5 **Hajj**, the pilgrimage to Makkah to be undertaken once in a lifetime if at all possible. Anyone who has performed Hajj may call him or herself a hajji.

Although it is possible for a Muslim to visit Makkah at any time of year, there is a particular month for undergoing Hajj. On this occasion millions of Muslims travel to Makkah, in Saudi Arabia. This is where the Kab'ah, a stone cube is built, around a black meteorite. Muslims believe the original Kab'ah was built by the prophet Ibrahim and his son, Ismail. It is in the centre of the mosque in Makkah and is the direction towards which all Muslims turn when they pray.

Male Muslims on Hajj wear special white robes called ihram or ahram, which are not hemmed as a sign of purity and that all Muslims are equal before Allah. Women wear simple black or white clothes and cover their heads.

The ritual involves walking anti-clockwise seven times (four times quickly then three times more slowly) around the Ka'bah and walking seven times back and forth between the Ka'bah and the Zamzam well where Hagar, Ibrahim's wife, found water to give to her son Ismail and so saved him from death. Muslims trace their ancestry back to Ibrahim, through Ismail, in the same way that Jews trace theirs back through Isaac.

Many will finish this part of the Hajj by drinking from the well.

They then camp at Mina, go to Arafat and return to Mina where there is a ceremony of stoning the devil. First, they stone one pillar or jamarat with seven pebbles. At this point a goat or sheep is sacrificed, a proportion of which is given to the poor. This sacrifice is a reminder of the story of Ibrahim and Ismail, where Allah appears to Ibrahim in a dream and asks him to sacrifice his son Ismail. Despite being tempted by the devil to disobey Allah, Ibrahim prepares to kill his son. At the last moment, Allah intervenes and provides a lamb for the sacrifice instead.

After the sacrifice is completed, the hajji throw stones at three pillars of stone. This stoning is repeated on the next day, too.

Anyone who has performed Hajj may call him or herself a hajji.

At the same time as the sacrifice is performed in Makkah, Muslims who have not gone on Hajj will arrange for an animal to be killed at home, usually by their local halal butcher. Part of the meat will be shared with the poor or money will be given to charity as an important part of this festival.

In other ways this Eid is celebrated like Eid ul-Fitr with a visit to the mosque for prayers, special foods shared with family and friends, and the exchange of cards and presents.

Christine Howard

Assembly theme: Celebrations

Most primary schools aim to introduce Reception children into assemblies gradually during the autumn term but, by Christmas, many try to bring everyone together to celebrate, often inviting parents as well. It's best to keep their involvement simple and, if possible, relate it to presenting work they have done in the classroom.

Music
Set the scene by playing recorded or live music as a signal for children to be quiet and ready to listen. You could use the same music every time or play some seasonal music or a favourite piece that gets everybody's feet tapping!

- *The Nutcracker Suite* by Tchaikovsky
- *Christmas Oratorio* by J S Bach
- Brazilian samba music
- 'Merry Christmas' by Slade
- 'I wish it could be Christmas' by Roy Wood.

Introduction
Invite a confident child to introduce the theme: 'We are going to show you some of our work on celebrations.'

Rhymes
Begin with a song or rhyme that involves all the children.

Try this finger rhyme about candles:

Four tall candles, shining bright *(Hold up four fingers)*
Burning with a yellow light *(Wiggle fingers)*
Choose one flame to blow away *(Blow)*
To celebrate this special day. *(Each child chooses one finger to bend over)*

Three tall candles, shining bright… *(Hold up three fingers)*

No tall candles, shining bright *(Hold up hand in fist)*
Burning with a yellow light

Preparation
- Teach the candles finger rhyme below and practise it individually and all together.
- Talk about celebrations and ask children to share their experiences of special occasions including birthdays, Christmas, anniversaries, Diwali, Chinese New Year, parties, weddings, new baby.
- Work with children in small groups to prepare mimes about celebrations.
- Make rangoli patterns using PVA glue and coloured sand or chalk.
- Practise telling the stories of Babouska and the Mexican posada.
- Make a Mexican piñata (see page 67).
- Make a Crown of King's. (See page 67.)
- Practise circle dances and celebration song.
- Learn the final song and add musical instruments.

Choose one flame to burn away *(Choose a finger to pop up)*
To celebrate this special day.

Mimes
Choose three or four small groups of children to perform short mimes about a celebration and invite the audience to guess what children are celebrating.

Birthday – Ask two children to stand up holding bunches of balloons. Use boxes covered in bright wrapping paper as presents. Children give them to the birthday boy or girl who opens the parcels and shows delight!

Diwali – Help two children to hold up strings of tinsel. Light some night lights and place in jam jars or use diva lamps.

Display rangoli patterns. Invite three or four children to mime arriving at a party and dancing.

Wedding – Two children dress up as bride and groom and walk slowly together as though walking up the aisle in church.

Ask children what other celebrations and festivals they enjoy at home.

Christmas celebrations around the world

Use the song 'Getting ready for Christmas' and the first two paragraphs. Explain that festivals are celebrated around the world in various ways. Choose two or three different countries to show. For more information about how Christmas is celebrated around the world see pages 66-68.

Dance

If you have the space, organise children into small circles and do a celebratory dance. Try simple side steps round the circle, to the right (count four), to the left (count four), step on the spot (count four), and wiggle on the spot. Use the tune to 'In and out the dusty bluebells' and sing:

> Come and join our celebration (x3)
> Celebration dance!

Quiet time

This can be in the form of a prayer or a time when children sit quietly, with eyes closed and hands in their laps to encourage them to listen and think about what they have heard. Ask them to say thank-you for celebrations and all the fun with friends and family that they bring.

Finale

Finish with a song involving all the children, such as 'Getting ready for Christmas' (see above) or any favourite seasonal carols and invite the audience to join in.

Judith Harries

Getting Ready for Christmas

Judith Harries

Chorus
Get - ting rea - dy for Christ - mas,___ Bells be - gin to ring,

Get - ting rea - dy for Christ - mas___ Join in now and sing.

Verse
Lights are twink - ling white and gold, Through the bran - ches

green and bold. As we de - co - rate the tree,

I see pre - sents for you and me!

Celebrating birthdays

Children look forward to their birthday and there are lots of ways that a child's special day can be celebrated at nursery or school.

For more confident children, being the centre of attention is an opportunity for them to share their news and talk about themselves. However, some children find it alarming to be singled out in any way. You need to be sensitive to this and pick the appropriate celebration for each child.

Birthday displays
Some settings have a display board showing everyone's birthdays. Children enjoy finding their name or picture on the board. Here are some simple ideas for designs. (List children's names inside each shape and/or use photographs.)

- 12 giant candles on a cake, one for each month
- 12 rockets or planets on a black background with silver stars
- 12 hot air balloons on a blue sky
- 12 presents cut out of wrapping paper.

On the day
Some children enjoy being 'helper for the day' or wearing a birthday crown. Others prefer a more low-key approach. You may want to share a birthday time with all the children together. In our nursery, at the end of the session we invite any children with birthdays to sit in the 'birthday chair', which is a simple, white, wooden chair, decorated with painted balloons. We invite the child's parents or carers to come early and join in.

The children take it in turns to choose their candles on the birthday board: an appliquéd picture of a birthday cake with space for up to five different coloured candles to be attached with Velcro. We also light candles for each child to blow out and take the opportunity to remind them about the dangers of matches. We use white household candles, standing them up in a piece of wood with holes drilled in for stability. After a rousing chorus of 'Happy Birthday' the birthday child is invited to blow out the candles and receives a birthday card from everyone.

Birthday treats
- Invite children to make a card for their friend's birthday.

- Give the child a special badge or sticker to wear all day.

- Invite the birthday child to choose a favourite story to be read out loud at snack time.

Jehovah's Witnesses do not recognise birthdays and may not want their children to join in birthday celebrations, for example singing 'Happy Birthday'. For more information, see pages 21-22.

- Make a birthday dice by sticking a song or rhyme to each of six sides of a cube. The birthday child rolls the dice and everyone sings the song that comes up on top.

Birthday songs and rhymes
Everyone knows the words and tune to 'Happy Birthday', so here are some other songs to try:

> Four bright candles on _____'s birthday cake
> Four bright candles on _____'s birthday cake
> I've counted them slowly, so there's no mistake,
> One, two, three, four
> Four bright candles on _____'s birthday cake.
> (Tune: 'Ten green bottles')

> Samuel has a birthday,
> Hip, hip, hip hooray.
> And on his cake he has five candles,
> Hip, hip, hip hooray.
> With a (blow, blow) here
> (Tune: 'Old Macdonald')

Birthday take-aways
Involve parents by sending home a 'Birthday bear' or 'Birthday bag'. The bear goes home overnight with the child in a plastic wallet together with a disposable camera and is returned the next day. The child can then tell the other children what they did and the photos can be displayed on the birthday board. The 'Birthday bag' can include picture books about birthdays together with a birthday book in which the child is invited to draw a picture and write about their special day. Include spare pages for siblings so the whole family gets involved!

Holiday birthdays
Children with school holiday birthdays miss out on all the fun so have a special day towards the end of each term when you celebrate all the holiday birthdays. Set up a group birthday tea or party and make a cake together.

Judith Harries

Birthday biscuits

You may copy this page to give parents so that they can share it with their child at home.

Help children to share their birthday with friends at nursery by making these tasty biscuits to eat at snack time!

You will need:

Plain shortbread
- 175g plain flour
- 125g butter or margarine
- 50g caster sugar.

Chocolate shortbread (or chocolate spread)
- 125g plain flour
- 75g butter or margarine
- 2 teaspoons of cocoa
- 50g caster sugar
- clean ice-lolly sticks.

- Make the plain shortbread first by rubbing the fat into the flour until it feels like breadcrumbs.

- Add the other ingredients and combine into a firm dough.

- Chill dough in the fridge while making the chocolate shortbread in the same way. Alternatively, spread chocolate spread onto the plain shortbread.

- Sprinkle the work surface with icing sugar.

- Roll out both types of dough into rectangles about 20 x 30cm.

- Place chocolate dough on top of the plain. Roll up from the narrow end like a Swiss roll!

- Cut into slices and put on baking trays.

- Push a lolly stick into each circle. Bake at 190C, gas mark 5 for 20 minutes.

If you find yourself with no time for cooking, try this short cut. Buy some plain digestive biscuits and let your child decorate them with tubes of different coloured squeezy icing!

Further resources

General RE for Foundation Stage

- *Handbook for RE in the Foundation Stage* (Solihull Metropolitan Borough Council) available from CSO Design and Print, Council House, Birmingham, B1 1BB. Tel: 0121 303 0064.

- Gift to the Child CD-Rom Available from Articles of Faith. Tel: 01992 454 636. Website: www.articlesoffaith.co.uk

Baha'i faith

- Baha'i National Office, 27 Rutland Gate, London, SW7 1PD. Tel: 0207 584 2566. Website: www.bahai.org.uk

Books about Birthdays:

- *Kipper's Birthday* Mick Inkpen (Hodder) ISBN 978-0-34093-206-3

- *Miffy's Birthday* Dick Bruna (Egmont) ISN 978-1-40521-023-2

- *Happy Birthday, Maisy* Lucy Cousins (Walker) ISBN 978-1-40630-691-0

- *Spot's Birthday* Party Eric Hill (Warne) ISBN 978-0-72326-414-9

Buddism

- *Under the Bodhi Tree – the story of Wesak* by Lynn Broadbent and John Logan (RMEP) ISBN 1-85175-204-8. Also available in big book format (RMEP) ISBN 1-85175-203-X.

- *My Buddhist Faith* by Adiccabandhu (Evans) ISBN 0-237-5179-8. Also available in big book format (Evans) ISBN 0-237-52214-4

Chinese New Year

- *Chinese New Year* by Catherine Chambers (Evans) ISBN 978-0-23754-118-7

- *The Great Race, the story of the Chinese Zodiac* retold by Dawn Casey (Barefoot Books Ltd.) ISBN 978-1-84686-077-5

Christmas

- *The Tallest Candle* (RMEP) Big book ISBN 978-1-85175-180-8, small version ISBN 978-1-85175-184-6

- *The Greatest Gift* (Barefoot Books) ISBN 978-1-84686-577-0

- Posada dolls (Mary and Joseph – from a Mexican custom) and animated video: Nicholas, the Boy who became Santa Both available from Articles of Faith Tel: 01992 454 636. Website: www.articlesoffaith.co.uk

- A range of nativity sets are also available from Articles of Faith. Tel: 01992 454 636. Website: www.articlesoffaith.co.uk

- For the classroom: Christmas cards with greetings in many languages, Advent calendar, DVD/video of the Christmas story.

Easter

- *A Very Special Sunday* by Lynne Broadbent and John Logan (RMEP) ISBN 978-1-81517-521-3. Also available as a big book (RMEP) ISBN 978-1-85175-212-6 and in a story bag from Articles of Faith.Tel: 01992 454 636. Website: www.articlesoffaith.co.uk

Islam

- *Muslim Nursery Rhymes* by Mustafa Yusuf McDermont (Islamic Foundation) ISBN 0-86037-342-8 available from Articles of Faith – a selection of Muslim nursery rhymes that can be sung to well-known tunes.

- *Marvellous Stories from the Life of Muhammad* by Mardijah Aldrich Tarantino (Islamic Foundation) ISBN 0-86037-103-4. Suitable as a teacher's resource.

- *Watching for the Moon* (RMEP) ISBN 978-1-85175-207-2

- *The Islamic Year* (Hawthorn Press) ISBN 978-1-90345-814-3

- For the classroom: Qur'an (in English/Arabic recommended rather than Arabic only), Ra'el (Qur'an stand), Qur'an cover.

Hinduism

- More details are available at the Hinduism for Schools website, managed by the Vivekananda Centre: www.hinduism.fsnet.co.uk

- www.hindunet.org

- www.hindukids.org

- www.hinduismtoday.com

Jehovah's Witnesses

- *Jehovah's Witnesses and Education*, a 32-page booklet (1995) written for non-Jehovah's Witness educators. Available from Watch Tower Bible and Tract Society of Britain.

- *Questions Young People Ask*, a 320-page book (1989) consisting of chapters on issues like 'School and work', written for younger Jehovah's Witnesses.

- *Jehovah's Witnesses and the School* (1997, 12 pages, £2.50) Redbridge Briefing Paper 2, Education Service, Lynton House, 255-259 High Road, Ilford, Essex 1G1 1NN.

Judaism

- The Board of Deputies of British Jews, 6 Bloomsbury Square, London, WC1A 2LP. Tel: 020 7543 5400. Website: www.bod.org.uk. E-mail: info@bod.org.uk

- The United Synagogue Agency for Jewish Education Bet Meir, 44a Albert Road, London, NW4 2SJ. Tel: 020 8457 9700. Website: www.aje.org.uk/index-jednet.htm E-mail: info@aje.org.uk

- DVD/Video: Ruth from the Testament series and soft toy versions of the lulav and etrog are available from Articles of Faith. Tel: 01992 454 636. Website: www.articlesoffaith.co.uk

Sikhism

- *Guru Nanak, a Birthday to Celebrate* by Lynn Broadbent and John Logan (RMEP). Sikh Gurdwara (A and C Black).

- Sikh Educational Advisory Services, Guru Guru House, 42 Park Avenue, Crossgates, Leeds, LS15 8EW.

Quakers

- Your local public library may have books about the Quakers and they will be able to tell you how to find your nearest Quaker meeting. Free booklets are available from: Quaker Life, Friends House, 173-177 Euston Road, London, NW1 2BJ. Tel: 020 7663 1000. Website: www.quaker.org.uk

Faiths and Festivals Book 1: A guide to the religions and celebrations in our multicultural society